OPENING THE GIFT

Rediscover
the Joy of Being Catholic

by Father Ed Eschweiler

HI-TIME PUBLISHING CORP. • BOX 13337 • MILWAUKEE, WI 53213

Scripture texts used in this book are taken from THE NEW AMERICAN BIBLE, copyright © 1970, with Revised New Testament, copyright © 1986, by the Confraternity of Christian Doctrine, Washington, DC, and are used with permission. All rights reserved.

Cover art by Joel Skaja
Typography and design by Sister Alice Ann Pfeifer, C.S.A.

Printed on recycled paper

HI-TIME Publishing Corp.
P.O. Box 13337
Milwaukee, WI 53213-0337

ISBN 0-937997-26-9

CONTENTS

ACKNOWLEDGEMENTS

Many people have contributed to this book. Most of them, I suspect, are not even aware of its existence. Some of these people are family, teachers--from grade school to post-graduate--and many others who have influenced me outside of the classroom through their lectures, writings, and tape recordings. They include, also, women and men with whom I studied, planned, and worked in parishes for a period of more than forty years. These people have shown me that God is always with us, gracious and also challenging; that all of creation is gift and trust; that faith is found, not in formulas but in the lives of people; and that religion is a matter not so much of rules but, rather, of relationships. In all of these, I believe, it is the Holy Spirit who spoke and guided.

Special thanks are due to my family and a circle of friends who have encouraged me in this effort and to the editors of HI-TIME Publishing Corporation for their assistance in the final editing.

Father Ed

FOREWORD

You have often heard the expression, "You can't beat experience." Father Ed Eschweiler has experience in the faith. For years he has lived it and tried to communicate to others what it is all about. It is difficult to beat his experience.

To experience the faith is, as he shows us, not enough. We must also be able to communicate what we have experienced. Some persons, like Father Ed, seem to be gifted in that capacity of communicating. Father Ed is masterful at saying what he believes, and he does it easily and simply. Being able to do this is a marvelous gift that comes only with age and experience.

Sometimes we can describe well what we believe, but we are not so capable of telling what we do not believe. Here, Father Ed is most helpful. He always points out what his faith is not all about. In that way we can easily follow him when he tells us what he truly believes as he helps us avoid the pitfalls along the way.

We are all concerned in this day and age with our Catholic heritage, what it is and what it means. Before we can live that heritage to the fullest, we must know what it stands for. This book will be of inestimable help to us. It articulates what that heritage is all about, and it does so in contemporary terms, post-Vatican II terminology we would say. It does not, however, falsify the deep verities that have made our Catholic tradition what it is. This book will be a fine guide to anyone seeking to pass on the faith and to anyone who has that awesome responsibility of explaining our faith to others.

Today, many persons, including parents and teachers, are asking for helps in teaching the basic truths of our faith. This book can be recommended without reserve. It is clear and deceptively simple. I say "deceptively simple" because Father Ed has the art of making complicated issues seem so natural, like breathing and eating and sleeping.

Faith, too, must become such an integral part of our lives and accompany every moment of our existence. It must permeate everything we do and think. It is a set of beliefs, but it is also a way of life and a way of seeing life. The way Father

Ed explains it all will help us communicate our faith. We will be freer in doing this at home, in school, and in the marketplace. We now sometimes call this aspect of our Christian vocation *evangelization*. We will become more confident evangelizers.

True faith grows more mellow and deeper with age. Rather than ask the tricky questions (such as "How many angels can dance on the head of a pin?"), we begin to ask the essential ones about the meaning of life and death and afterlife. "How does this world and what we do here affect that other world beyond that we are destined for?" Faith does not always have easy answers to these probing issues, but it gives us the framework within which to answer for ourselves.

Some persons might ask, "Why not just read the Bible?" This is a good question. No book is a substitute for the Bible; Catholics must never forget that truth. But people who have lived with the Bible in hand also have wisdom to contribute to us. From their enviable experience of living daily with the word of God, they have a way of seeing life and of seeing the truths of the faith as expressed in the Bible.

Books of wisdom and belief such as this one by Father Eschweiler will help us enter more fully into the Bible and into the whole of the Church's tradition. We will see how generations have lived the discipleship of Christ that is described in the Bible, and we will be introduced to the deep reflections about life that such believers have evolved.

A faith that is not lived is indeed a dead faith. Reading a book such as this will help each of us reflect on how well we are carrying out the demands of our faith. The book will be a constant reminder of how much we have to learn and also of how much we have yet to do.

We are grateful that Father Ed Eschweiler took time out to share with us his years of experience in living the faith. What a singular and blessed gift!

Most Reverend Rembert G. Weakland, O.S.B.
Archbishop of Milwaukee

1

THE GOD I BELIEVE IN

Dear Friends,

In my years as a priest, I have not met many people who claimed to be atheists, but I have met many whose gods I do not believe in. These are gods with all-seeing eyes, not so much to watch over, to care for, but to watch for, to check up on. These are gods with computer-like minds, storing for instant retrieval all the deeds, especially the bad deeds of people.

I don't believe in gods who punish harshly, who give people a rough time on earth as a way of their earning a good time in heaven. I don't believe in a god who created the earth, flung it spinning into space and left it and all those upon it on their own. There are many more gods I don't believe in, but I would like most of all to reflect on the God I do believe in.

The God I believe in is the God of creation. The God I believe in is an artist whose works are works of beauty. The breathtaking beauty of sunrises and sunsets, of the nighttime sky. God's artistry creates the beauty of wooded hills, of streams and lakes, of a single leaf or raindrop or delicate blossom.

The God I believe in, my friends, loves man and woman; God made them. Like a potter with clay in hand, with care and love, God made them. God shaped their bodies, located and gave function to their internal organs. The God I believe in shaped their bones, their muscles, their sinews, gave texture to their skin and curves to their limbs. Male and female God made them. God gave each of them qualities that would attract and sustain the other. Sex and all the ways that men and women complement one another physically, emotionally, and spiritually were God's idea from the beginning.

God is playful, making so many funny and surprising things.

The God I believe in gives us eyes--eyes to see, to speak with sometimes, to twinkle, and to laugh. God gives us ears to hear the whisper of the breeze, the lapping of the waves, the crackling of a fire, the singing of the birds, the music that we ourselves can make, the voices of those we love.

The God I believe in gives us hands--hands that can do all kinds of work, that can take canvas and clay and fashion them into works of art. Hands that can be lent to another to help and support. Hands that can touch, caress, and hold another person.

God gives us nerves that can sense, that respond with pleasure to sources of enjoyment, that respond also with pain to sources of harm and destruction.

God gives us a mind that can know and, no matter how much it knows, can still learn more. A mind that can understand what already is and an imagination to conceive and plan, dream about and invent what is not yet. A mind whose highest thoughts are a reflection of the God who made us. And God also gives us a heart. A heart that can love and can always grow in loving--loving all that God loves and all that God is.

The God I believe in gives us a spirit that has life, loves life, gives life. A spirit in constant quest for what is beyond, for the infinite. A spirit that, as St. Augustine says, is restless until it finds rest in the infinite God.

God gives us a sense of humor; the ability to see the

incongruous and ridiculous in things, in events, in others and, most important, in ourselves.

The God I believe in likes birds and bugs, butterflies and bees. In fact, God likes them so much it seems God could hardly stop making new and different ones. God is playful, making so many funny and surprising things. Birds and flowers, animals and fish and people!

The God I believe in likes colors. And so, God made many of them with infinite variations in shade, and splashes them lavishly throughout creation on birds and bugs, fish and rocks, sunsets and flowers. The God I believe in likes natural things; God made them. And God likes beautiful things; they reflect God.

The God I believe in likes changing seasons and changing weather, light and shadow, water and land, warm sun and cool breezes. But it seems to me, God has a special liking for water, spreading it around in creation in so many ways: rain coming down, springs coming up, rivers and lakes. And as if all this is not enough, God conceived a whimsical form of water--snow. God can stack snow up, hang it on trees, sculpture it with the wind. With snow, God can give to water an entirely new function and form of beauty.

The God I believe in, friends, is also the God of Scripture. Most of all, the God of Scripture loves people, body-spirit people. In the beginning, God walks with them in the cool of the day. That's the time after work when friends get together. And when the people betray God's friendship, God doesn't stop being a friend to them. The God I believe in will not give vent to blazing anger, simply because God is God and not a human person. God is a God of compassion, who hears the cry of the poor, who will not crush the bruised reed or quench the smoldering wick, who promises to keep vigil with people on their journey. The God I believe in promises that even if a mother should forget her child, God will not forget us.

The God I believe in is also a God who challenges: challenges us to have faith, who promises a child to Abraham and Sarah when they are too old to have children, who asks them to move to an unknown land, who promises a future blessing. And God keeps those promises.

9

In the fullness of time, God sends God's own Son to be born of one of us. Jesus, the Son, becomes one with us. He walks the countryside, goes to the cities where the people are. He takes children into His arms and hugs them. He tenderly gives back a dead son, now alive again, to his widowed mother. He gives health to the sick and food to the hungry who follow Him.

When the time comes to end His life on earth, He invents new ways to be with us. He tells us that He will be here in the community of His followers. He is here when we come together to remember Him in the breaking of the bread. Before He leaves, He does one more thing for us: He gives us His mother to be our mother.

The God I believe in, friends, is quite a God, a God who is ours, whenever we're ready.

Peace!

Father Ed

QUESTIONS FOR REFLECTION OR DISCUSSION

1. Has your concept of God changed since you were a child? In what ways?
2. What influences have helped, or could help, you acquire a new and better understanding of God? Life experiences--both painful and joyful? Reading the Bible? Participating in a small group for Bible study and faith sharing?

2

THE JESUS I BELIEVE IN

Dear Friends,

Our faith tells us that Jesus is most mysterious: true God and true man. How can this be? We don't know. What does this mean on the practical level? Again, we don't know for sure. When Jesus spoke to the crowds on the hillsides and plains of Galilee, did He amplify His voice miraculously so that they could hear Him? I don't think so. Remember how on one occasion Jesus told the disciples to gather the people into groups of fifty? I think He could speak to fifty and be heard. Then He could move on to another group.

St. Paul tells us that Jesus was like us in all things except sin. In being born of Mary, Jesus accepted all the aches and pains, all the feelings of joy and sorrow, all the human limitations, emotions, and temptations that you and I experience. In this letter, I'd like to tell you a little about the Jesus I see in the Gospels, the Jesus I believe in.

Jesus was a man. Although I believe that He is also the unique Son of God, what I see in the Gospels, most of all, is a man. Not just the appearance of a man, but one who is fully human.

He was born. This means that He was, first of all, a helpless infant. Then a child. As a child, He learned and, like us, He sometimes learned by His mistakes. He was not merely any kind of a child; He was a boy. That means He got Himself

11

dirty, and He got His clothes dirty. It means that He tore His clothes sometimes when He played. And He tore His skin sometimes when He fell.

Did Jesus run away from His home and family? The Gospels do not put it that way, but at the age of twelve, He stayed behind in Jerusalem when His family left for home in Nazareth. Three days later, when they found Him in the Temple, He returned home with them. It seems to me that relationships in the household of Joseph, Mary, and Jesus could never be the same after that. The little boy Jesus was becoming the young man Jesus. The Gospels do not tell us about this period or what the homelife in Nazareth was like. It sums up the next eighteen years or so very simply: He grew in wisdom and age and grace before God and man.

He was a part of His community....

Jesus was not only a man but a Jewish man, and a man of His time, His people, and His land. He thought like the Jews of His time. He spoke like them, even with a Galilean accent. Like a good Jew, Jesus was a remembering person. He was conscious of the history of His people. Like a good Jew, He studied the Scriptures. He frequently mentioned the great figures of Jewish history. He felt like a Jew. Like a good Jew, Jesus prayed the Psalms. He went to the community prayer houses, the synagogues. He was a part of His community, and the Gospels tell us He was an active participant in it.

Jesus apparently moved out on His own, probably as a young adult. He moved from Nazareth to the town of Capernaum. Here, I assume, He carried on in His father's trade as a carpenter. Carpentry is hard work today; it was harder then. So, Jesus would be strong, especially in His hands and arms. He would know wood and, I think, love it. He would know its feel, its look, its smell. When He looked at a tree, He couldn't help seeing not only a tree, a tree that gives shade or figs, but also a tree that gives lumber. He would see the things that could be made from the wood of that tree. In His last months, it seems to me, when He saw a tree, He could not help seeing a cross!

Jesus displayed a capacity for human emotions, for love and anger and compassion. He not only loved children; He also showed that love in a human way. He put His arms around them and embraced them. He loved His twelve apostles. He defended them when they were attacked by the scribes and Pharisees. He took them away for a day off when they were tired after a missionary journey of their own. It is true that He grew impatient with their slowness to learn and their petty maneuvering for the first places in His kingdom, but He loved them. And at the Last Supper He made this remarkable statement: He would no longer call them servants but friends. And the reason was that He had told them everything.

Jesus also had women friends, Martha and Mary. He liked going to their home just to visit and to share a meal. I like to think of their home as His "get-away"--the place where He could go to relax and be refreshed for His ministry. He also loved Lazarus, their brother, not as one of His apostles, a co-worker, but just as a friend. And, in one of the more touching scenes in the Gospels, we read that when Lazarus died, Jesus came to the tomb and wept.

Jesus had a capacity for tenderness and compassion. He would reach out and touch the diseased and suffering who came or were brought to him. And He healed many. It strikes me that it wasn't just the fact that Jesus healed them but also the way that He did it that was important. He touched them, their eyes, their ears. In a very human way, He showed them that He loved them. He was compassionate with the spiritually ill, too, the sinners. He attracted the outcasts of His world because they sensed that He would not cast them out.

He also had a capacity for anger. He overturned the tables of the money-changers in the Temple. He lost all patience with scribes and Pharisees. He called them a family of snakes. He said they were like fancy-looking graves full of rottenness inside. He was angry with them for their pretense of religion, their self-righteousness. He was angry that their teaching of religion imposed heavy burdens on God's people

13

and that they did nothing to lighten those burdens. He was angry that their teaching emphasized minute details of ritual laws and often neglected the bigger issues of justice and mercy. He was angry with them for their failure to love.

The Gospels show us that Jesus was close to the lives of His people. He loved to use examples from their experience to teach us about Himself and His Father. This would show us how we should relate to Him, to His Father and to one another. He says that He is like a shepherd caring for sheep and searching for one that is lost. He speaks of God's word in stories about a farmer who sows a field and about a farmer who is plagued with weeds. He tells us God is like a woman (yes, a woman!) who loses a coin and sweeps the whole house in search of it. He tells of how she rejoices when she finds it. God, He tells us, is like that with us when we are sinners, "lost," and are found and come back to God. He teaches about the coming of the kingdom of God in terms of a woman baking bread and the silent, mysterious, and transforming action of the leaven.

With a touch of humor, He likes to exaggerate things to the point of making them sound ridiculous. In that way we will not easily forget what He is teaching. He tells us, for example, to take the beam (I always think of a telephone pole) out of our own eye, before we try to take the speck out of our neighbor's. He accuses the Pharisees of straining out a gnat but swallowing a whole camel. (The camel was probably the largest animal in their experience.) He wants us not to let our left hand know what charity our right hand does.

As a teacher, Jesus was concerned that people get the correct image of His Father. He was concerned that they not confuse hygiene, things like washing one's hands before eating, with religion. He wanted them to understand that laws, even the most sacred Sabbath laws, are made for people and not the other way around.

Jesus notices little things. He notices things like the lilies of the field and the sparrows. He does not mention the fancy flowers and birds; He talks about the ordinary ones. He notices things like people reading the sky in the evening to tell what tomorrow's weather will be. He notices the way the

Pharisees lengthen their phylacteries to show off and the way the guests seek the places of honor when they are invited to a meal. Jesus also notices the "little people," like fishermen and day-laborers. The outcasts of society, like lepers and prostitutes. The poor, the sick, and widows. Those who were powerless and, because they were powerless, often ignored. He went about among all of these doing good.

Most of all, He loves His Father. He can say, "I do always the things that please the Father." And He wants more than anything else that we come to see His Father as our Father, too. And that we come to love His Father as He does.

There is, of course, much more that can be said about Jesus, but this is something of a picture of the Jesus I believe in. I hope and pray that Jesus, fully divine and fully human, may become ever more real, ever more a personal friend for each of us!

Peace!

Father Ed

QUESTIONS FOR REFLECTION OR DISCUSSION

1. How can it help us to think of Jesus as fully human when we are tempted? When we are tired or discouraged? When we are sick? In what other situations?
2. Name some human characteristics of Jesus, from this letter or from the Gospels, that help you relate to Him.

3

THE SPIRIT I BELIEVE IN

Dear Friends,

When we talk about God--Father, Son and Holy Spirit--
we know deep down that our understanding is immensely
inadequate and our words are even more so. When we studied
about God in philosophy, we used a twofold process. First, we
affirmed of God a positive quality, like goodness. Then we
denied of God all the imperfections we see in the goodness of
people around us. So far, so good. Even then, however, we
must confess that we are far from coming to the full truth of
who God is. But we do the best we can do, until....

There is a story about St. Thomas Aquinas, surely one of
the most profound and prolific theological writers of all time.
Near the end of his life, he had an experience of God and he
never wrote again. He said that everything he had written
was like straw.

So, friends, straw it may be, pearls of wisdom it surely
will not be, but I write simply to share with you some
thoughts on the Spirit I believe in. And I trust that, at least in
some sense, the Holy Spirit, the Spirit of Truth, will be with
me as I do so.

A couple of years ago, at a parishioner's family gathering, I met a young woman who had recently come to Milwaukee from somewhere in Michigan. She was a professionally
trained social worker. In the course of the evening, she told

me this story. She said the Spirit had prompted her to make the change. She had not known anyone in Milwaukee and had hardly any knowledge of the city. She came, as she understood it, in obedience to the Spirit's prompting. After arriving, she was unable for some time to find employment in her profession. One evening, seeking further guidance from God, she opened her Bible, closed her eyes and, without looking, placed a finger on the page. The text her finger rested on was in the Book of Revelation and it reads, "Do the works you did at first" (Revelation 2:5). She went on to explain that before she finished her education she had been a keypunch operator. She understood that this Bible text was the guidance she was seeking. She then looked for and found a position in that kind of work. All this--her leaving her home in Michigan, her moving to Milwaukee, her return to being a keypunch operator--was, she said, at the direction of the Holy Spirit.

I do not believe in such a Spirit.

When I was in the seminary, Latin was a major subject of study. One of the phrases we used frequently in a joking way was *dabitur vobis*; this means, "It will be given to you." It comes from an occasion when Jesus was re-assuring His disciples. He told them not to be afraid when they were persecuted. The Spirit would give them what they were to say. (See Matthew 10:19.) We used to apply this to ourselves when we were not properly prepared for an exam: "Don't worry" was the idea, "even if you didn't do your preparation, it will be given to you!"

I do not believe in that kind of a Spirit, either.

Describing the role of the Spirit in these ways is to deny something that is very important to human dignity: personal responsibility. I believe God wants us to use the gifts God gives us: our intelligence, our experience, our judgment, our free will, and the wisdom of others, gathered in a life of openness to the Spirit. The Spirit I believe in works in all of us as we do what we can in our human situations.

Sometime ago I participated in a small faith-sharing group. At one point, one of the members asked, "When you pray, do you pray to God as Father, or to Jesus, or to the Holy Spirit?" Some answered that they prayed to God without referring in a specific way to any of the Persons. Others said that they prayed to the Father as we all do, for example, in the Lord's Prayer. Finally, some said that they found it easiest to pray to Jesus because they can picture Jesus in scenes from the Gospels. Not one of them mentioned praying to the Holy Spirit.

This, friends, caught me by surprise, although perhaps it should not have. We all have images of fathers. It is easy for us to picture Jesus because we hear and read the Gospels so frequently. But how can we imagine the Holy Spirit? This "new" name, *Holy Spirit*, is better than *Holy Ghost* but it still is too "spiritual," too abstract. We have knowledge and experience of fathers and sons, but we have no experience of persons who are spirits. We cannot see the Holy Spirit. I'm afraid that, in our minds, Spirit--even with a capital S--is rather close to unreal.

When I instructed religion classes in parish schools, I sometimes used a book as a kind of fan and, with a rapid swing, created a wind that the students could feel. They could not see the wind but could sense that it was real. Then we would talk about breezes and different kinds of winds. We would talk about breezes that propel boats across the sea and storm winds that create great waves. We talked about winds that cause topsoil to blow away and winds that shape new-fallen snow into exquisitely beautiful drifts. We know, too, that winds can drive turbines which generate electricity and do it without consuming precious fossil fuels or producing pollution.

Like the wind I created with the book in the classroom and the different kinds of breezes and winds in nature, the Spirit I believe in is real.

I think I will always remember an experience I had when I was being transferred from one parish to another. A woman came up to me and asked if I remembered the time I had visited her family at home. I said I did. She went on to ask me whether I remembered what I had said at that time, but I did not. She told me what it was, but I still had no recollection of having said it. Then she said, "Father, if you had not said that, you would never have seen us in church again." I can only say that it was the Spirit who prompted my remark.

The Spirit I believe in has a special voice that speaks without words or sounds, but directly to the heart. We call it inspiration. In the very beginning of the Bible, in the story of creation, we read that a mighty wind swept over the waters. Mighty wind here could also be translated "wind of God" or "breath of God." Some translations--the Jerusalem Bible, for example--use the word *Spirit*. When God shaped the body of the first man out of the clay of the ground, God blew into his nostrils the breath of life, and so the man became a living being. Think of that, friends--God's breath became the breath of the man! (See Genesis 2:7.)

The Spirit I believe in gives life, natural life first of all, but also the new life we have as Christians, our SPIRIT-ual life. That life begins when we are baptized in the name of the Father and of the Son and of the Holy Spirit. This life is, first of all, a life of faith. It is only in the Spirit that we become believers who are able to say Jesus is Lord. (See 1 Corinthians 12:3.) And it is the Spirit who enables us to understand that we are God's children and can call God *Abba*, which means "father," "dad," or "daddy." (See Romans 8:15.) When Jesus tells us that we should speak to God as Father, He is telling us to pray in the Holy Spirit.

I do not always find it easy to pray, but I always ask the Spirit to help. Even then, I sometimes realize that I just can't pray as I ought, and then I simply ask the Spirit within me to pray my prayer for me. (See Romans 8:26-27.) When I do pray, the Spirit is my guide; when I cannot pray, the Spirit I believe in is my advocate. The Spirit I believe in is love. When we are able to love one another, it is the Spirit who enables us to do so. Perhaps at times we all find it difficult to love others--individual persons or groups. I know I do. Some of them seem so "different." When I realize this, it helps me to recall that different people have different gifts, but we all receive them from the same Spirit. (See 1 Corinthians 12:4.)

The Spirit I believe in makes our love practical and effective. When Jesus stood up to give His inaugural address in the synagogue in Nazareth, He said:

"The Spirit of the Lord is upon me,
   because he has anointed me...
to proclaim liberty to captives
   and recovery of sight to the blind,
      to let the oppressed go free."

Luke 4:18

The Spirit I believe in is peace and forgiveness--above all, God's forgiveness in the sacrament of Penance, Rite of Reconciliation. On the first Easter Sunday, the Risen Lord appeared to His frightened disciples, who were huddled behind locked doors in the upper room. He greeted them: "Peace be with you....Receive the Holy Spirit. Whose sins you forgive are forgiven them..." (John 20:21-22). The Spirit I believe in is also the peace and forgiveness men and women, groups and nations offer each other. The most common symbol for the Holy Spirit is the dove, and the dove is the most common symbol for peace.

The Spirit I believe in is courage and strength. After Luke's account in the Acts of the Apostles of the coming of the Spirit on Pentecost, the disciples, previously so timid and fearful, boldly go out and preach the Risen Lord. They preach in the power of the Spirit. (See Acts 2:3-4.) When Pope John XXIII announced the Second Vatican Council, he composed a prayer asking the Holy Spirit: "Renew Your wonders by a new Pentecost in our time." It was an exciting time in the Church. One young man said of me--he didn't say it to me but to others about me--that the council gave me a new lease on life. And he was right! I recall the times quite clearly. I read everything I could find on the preparations for the council and on the deliberations of the bishops during their meetings.

Even so, I do not think that anyone expected that the opening of the windows of the Church to let in fresh air, the wind of God, would so transform the Church. Like the first Pentecost, the Second Vatican Council was an experience of the power of the Holy Spirit, a new understanding of who we are as the Church of Christ and a new vision of what we are called to do, not only in the Church, but in the modern world. It was a time of *enthusiasm*, a word which comes from two

Greek words for *in* and *God*. To be enthusiastic is to be in God or to be aware that God is in us and that we are possessed by God. The Second Vatican Council took us all by surprise. The Spirit I believe in is the surprise of God.

The Spirit I believe in is the light that dispels the darkness, the fire of love that displaces hatred and apathy, the truth and honesty that overcomes deception and the playing of games. The Spirit I believe in replaces sadness and emptiness with joy and happiness. The Spirit removes meaninglessness and depression and infuses purpose and zest. The Spirit I believe in moves us from unbelief to faith and brings life and renewal where otherwise there would be only death and decay. The Spirit I believe in is a gift from Jesus. This gift is given in His dying breath. (See John 19:30.) We might say that the Spirit is the dying wish of Jesus for all of us. In my years as a priest, I have often heard people talk about the dying wish of a parent or other relative or friend. Such a wish has a special hold on us. We see it as a sacred trust. Gifts, too, given by a person shortly before death, are especially treasured. The Spirit is the gift Jesus gives to us as He dies on the cross. From that time on, friends, we live in the age of the Spirit.

May my prayer, the Church's prayer, be your prayer, too: "Send forth your Spirit and renew the face of the earth."

Peace!

Father Ed

QUESTIONS FOR REFLECTION OR DISCUSSION

1. Why is it important for us to foster our relationship with the Holy Spirit?
2. Think of some examples of the action of the Holy Spirit in your life.
3. Discuss this statement: If Christians had a better understanding of and relationship with the Holy Spirit, there would be more joy in their lives.

4

THE BIBLE I BELIEVE IN

Dear Friends,

The Bible is not only a perennial best seller. It is a book whose words millions of people all over the world strive to live by. It is studied, researched, translated, memorized, used in prayer, and revered by millions of people as the word of God. It is at the heart of our faith. Even so, many people have never been taught much about how to read and understand it. I appreciate the opportunity to tell you a little about the Bible I believe in and to give you some insights into how to understand this unique literary and religious treasure.

There are Bibles, my friends, that I don't believe in. I don't, for instance, believe in a Bible which is dictated by God to the inspired author, like a letter that a business executive dictates to a secretary. I don't believe in Scriptures which are to be pulled apart, with isolated texts used almost like a club to win an argument. I don't believe in a Bible that calls for a literal understanding in the sense that it means all and only what it says on the surface. I don't believe in a Bible that will answer all of our questions, solve all of our problems, and cure all of our ills.

Most of all, though, I want to tell you about the Bible I do believe in. The Bible I believe in is God's word--God's word in the language of men and women. The work of the human authors is not just the writing down. Their work is truly the work of authorship. Their personalities, literary styles, and experiences shape the text. I used to think that when we say the Bible is the word of God, it means that God simply put the ideas into the authors' heads. Today, we see it differently. The authors, reflecting on their own experiences and, even more, on the experiences of their people, see the action of God in them. The Israelites were chosen by God, who promised to be with them. We believe that God was with them in their great experiences and in their reflecting and writing about those experiences. We believe that God is with all of us, also, as we read, reflect, and pray over these writings.

Because the authors brought their own personalities, styles, and experiences to their writing, we can see that the more we know about the people and the times of these writings, the more we will understand what the authors meant. In 1943, Pope Pius XII wrote that in reading and studying the Bible, we must "go back wholly in spirit to those remote centuries of the East." Because the Bible is also God's word, what the author meant is what God is saying to us.

The authors of the Bible I believe in often used language which had not only an obvious meaning but also another meaning, a deeper one, which was not so obvious. There is the story of Jesus curing a man born blind. At the end of the account, we can see that the story is not only about physical blindness. It is also about an even greater evil. It is about the blindness of refusing to believe in Jesus.

Again, light and darkness, day and night have obvious meanings. In the Bible I believe in, they can also have symbolic meanings. Light and day are symbols of all that is good. Darkness and night are symbols of all that is evil. If we understand this, then we will find that a very short sentence in the Gospel according to St. John is tremendously powerful and moving. It is in the account of the Last Supper. Jesus has just washed the feet of the disciples. Then, deeply troubled, He announces that one of them is a traitor. Shortly after this, Judas leaves the Supper and goes out to betray his Lord. What could be more evil? The Gospel then gives us this very short sentence, four words, a total of four syllables: "And it was night" (John 13:30). Clearly, John is not merely telling us the time of day. He is telling us that this is an evil time.

The Bible--the word means "book"--is really a collection of books. It is a library. The authors of these books lived in different periods of history, covering a span of probably more than a thousand years. The latest of them wrote approximately eighteen hundred years ago. It is interesting and important to realize, also, that many of these books were written by one person and at a later time were edited, added to, and revised by others. In a very real sense, the Bible comes to us from a people--a people of faith. And it was written for a people of faith. From faith to faith. Together, the books of the Bible form a diary, or perhaps more accurately, a journal, a book of memoirs of God's people.

These books include different kinds of writing. Perhaps the easiest way to think of this is to think of a daily newspaper. The paper has sections of news. The important things in the news sections will become a part of recorded history. The paper also has an editorial page. This does not describe things as they are, but as the writer thinks they ought to be. The paper has a weather forecast, an attempt to predict the future. It may also have an advice column. These are different kinds of literature, and we read them differently. The Bible also has different kinds of literature, and we should read them differently.

The Bible...is about a people who came to know the presence of God in their lives.

Much of what is recounted in the newspaper can be described adequately in simple, direct language. We can state, for instance, what the president said, where he was when he said it, and when the event took place. But there are other realities which cannot be put into words so simply. How would you express the experience of meeting a very important person? How would you describe being free after a long

24

imprisonment? How can one put into words what it is like to be loved? The Bible is about many things and it is very much about these three kinds of experiences. It is about a people who came to know the presence of God in their lives. It is about a people who were led to freedom. It is about a people whose life is a love story, a story of God's love for us!

When people have those kinds of experiences, they realize they cannot express them in ordinary language. They then try to describe them in poetry, in figures of speech, in stories. This is what we find in the Bible. I remember a theologian once remarking about people sometimes asking, "Did Jesus really walk on water? His reply was, "Don't you know that Jesus is always walking on water?" To understand what he is saying, we need to try to think like the Hebrews. In their way of thinking, creation was not God's making the world out of nothing but rather the taming of the waters of chaos. The deluge, in the story of Noah, was so frightening because the waters seemed again to be out of control. This would be the undoing of creation! Only God has that kind of power over water.

Another story that can help us understand the answer of that theologian is in the Gospel. Jesus was asleep in a boat when a sudden storm came up. The apostles panicked and called the Lord. "He woke up, rebuked the wind, and said to the sea: 'Quiet! Be still!' The wind ceased and there was a great calm" (Mark 4:39). We can sense their wonder and awe as they said to one another, "Who then is this whom even wind and sea obey?" (Mark 4:41).

When we think of these experiences, and how only God has that kind of power over the waters, we can see what the theologian means when he says that Jesus is always walking on water.

The story of the Exodus of the Israelites from Egypt and the crossing of the Reed Sea is another story of experiencing God's power over the waters. But it is primarily a story of how God brings the Jewish people to freedom. In our country, we have a tradition of freedom, and it is a highly prized value in our culture. We remember and celebrate it especially on the Fourth of July. In the Bible, God's people recount how God came to their rescue, leading them from slavery in Egypt to freedom in the promised land. They tell the story over and over in exuberant ways--in stories, in poetry, in sung prayer. For example:

> I will sing to the LORD, for he is gloriously
> triumphant;
> horse and chariot he has cast into
> the sea...
> The flood waters covered them,
> they sank into the depths like a stone.
>
> Exodus 15:1-5

God is always leading us to freedom.

Most of all, my friends, the Bible is a love story, a story of God's love for us. The story is told in many ways. One of these is in the book of Hosea. Hosea, the prophet, marries a prostitute, Gomer. After bearing several children, she goes back to her old ways. Hosea seeks her out and brings her home. Finally, Hosea comes to realize that he is living out in his own life God's experiences with the people. They are repeatedly unfaithful to their covenant. Even so, God continues to love them. God speaks of them as a bride:

> So I will allure her;
> I will lead her into the desert
> and speak to her heart.
>
> Hosea 2:16

Later, God says:

> My heart is overwhelmed,
> my pity is stirred.
> I will not give vent to my blazing anger...
> For I am God and not man.
>
> Hosea 11:8-9

The story of God's love is told finally and definitively in Jesus: God so loved the world that God sent the Son. When that Son, Jesus, talks about the kingdom of heaven, the ultimate relationship of love, He never tries to give a newspaper-type account. He always uses similes: The kingdom of heaven is like a mustard seed. It is like a treasure hidden in a field. It is like a pearl of great price. And the kingdom on earth leads to a heavenly banquet, a great feast in heaven! We are told that we cannot even imagine what things are prepared for those who love God.

The Bible I believe in, the word of God, not only *tells* us of God's love for us, it *does* things. The very first book of the Bible, the Book of Genesis, pictures God as speaking a word and all creation happens. There is also a beautiful passage about the power of God's word in the Book of Isaiah:

> For just as from the heavens
> the rain and snow come down
> And do not return there
> till they have watered the earth,
> making it fertile and fruitful,
> Giving seed to him who sows
> and bread to him who eats,
> So shall my word be
> that goes forth from my mouth:
> It shall not return to me void,
> but shall do my will,
> achieving the end for which I sent it.
>
> Isaiah 55:10-11

The Bible I believe in, my friends, is God's self-revelation, God's autobiography. It is also our faith-family history. It is the record of God's action in the world and of our successes and failures in response. It is the biographies of our great and not-so-great ancestors in faith. It is instruction and guide for us, invitation, encouragement, and nourishment for our journey. It is a word of experiencing God, a freeing word, a word of love. What more can one say: It is God's word.

Peace!

Father Ed

27

QUESTIONS FOR REFLECTION OR DISCUSSION

1. Do you think the Bible is easy to read and understand? Why or why not?

2. Many parishes list the citations for the Scripture readings for the days of the week in the Sunday bulletin. Think of ways you could use these readings by yourself, in the family, or in a discussion group, to grow in the knowledge and the living of God's word.

5

THE CHURCH I BELIEVE IN

Dear Friends,

Many things have changed in the Church since the Second Vatican Council, and the media keep telling us that many other things are being discussed and challenged.

There are Churches I used to believe in but do not anymore. The Church, for example, that has all the answers. In that Church, at least in the minds of some people, the Pope, the bishops, "Father" and "Sister" knew it all and you had better believe it. "Creeping infallibility" someone called it. Or the Church of many rules which gave rise to the description "strict Catholic." Sometimes in that Church the distinctions about the relative importance of various issues became blurred and "Thou shalt not talk in church" came across as not much different from "Thou shalt not bear false witness against thy neighbor." In some ways it almost seemed that that Church was better at getting you into sin than out of it.

And then there is the Church that is necessary for salvation, so the rectory becomes a kind of spiritual fire station with a priest always on duty, ready to rush out with his special prayers and holy oil to snatch some dying soul from the devil. I can't believe in that kind of Church because it speaks about a God I can't believe in. There are other Churches, too, I can't believe in, but I'd rather write about the Church I do believe in.

The Church I believe in is people. It is an organization, of course, with a hierarchy, structure, and obligations, but that's so that these people can work together and serve one another's needs better. So, the Church is people--people who share a faith in God and Jesus. They don't all understand everything in exactly the same way, but they have some basic beliefs in common. The Church I believe in is all the people who share these beliefs and who identify themselves within a tradition, which, for you and me, is the Catholic tradition. When I say all, I am emphasizing that it is not just the Pope, bishops, priests, and sisters. The Church I believe in is *all*, and the Pope and those others are not any more Church than you or I.

So the Church is always ambiguous: It is inspiring and disappointing, encouraging and frustrating....

One of the most amazing events in recent Church history took place on February 20, 1946. Pope Pius XII was presiding at the investiture of a group of new cardinals. These men had just been elevated to a position of great honor. They would be the ones to choose the next Pope, who would almost certainly be one of their number. And to these men, in this solemn consistory, Pius XII chose to speak about the laity; he said that they must come to a realization not only of belonging to the Church but also of being the Church. The people, who are the Church I believe in, are a holy people because God has called them and made them God's in a special way. But none of these people lives in a holy way all the time. So, the people who are the Church, who are holy, are also sinners. At our parish, when newcomers stop in to register, I always tease them. I explain that we are very strict, that we have one qualification for membership in our parish from which there are no exceptions. Sometimes they look very concerned for a moment. Then I explain: They must be sinners. If they weren't sinners, I say, they would make the rest of us, who are, very uncomfortable. So the Church is always ambiguous: It is inspiring and disappointing, encouraging and frustrating, simultaneously holy and sinful, already and not yet. In biblical terms, the Church is a pilgrim people--on the way, but not yet there.

At the beginning of a parish Sunday liturgy recently, this exchange took place between two readers:

"Do you like yourself?"
"Yes!"
"Are you satisfied with yourself?"
"No!"

And that is the way we who are the Church, who are holy and sinful, redeemed but not yet fully saved, good but not perfect, ought to feel about ourselves. We should like ourselves but not be satisfied.

In the Church I believe in, even though we are a sinful people, we are not obsessed with sin--with sin in general or with sinfulness in ourselves. We know that God is a loving father, or mother, if you wish. This loving God forgives us even when we find it difficult to forgive ourselves. In the Church I believe in, we who are these sinful but forgiven people can learn to forgive ourselves. And, after that, we can begin to forgive one another. How often? Peter suggested seven times to Jesus. Peter was being generous because in that culture seven was a symbolic number connoting perfection. Jesus replied, "Not seven times, but seventy times seven times." That's four hundred and ninety. But I am sure Jesus doesn't want us to carry a book or a ledger in a purse or a pocket and keep count.

The Church I believe in is not so much for people's salvation. I believe God takes care of that. Besides if that's what the Church is all about, it's a pretty sad failure. The latest figure I've seen is that less than twenty percent of the world's population is Catholic. Even if you add all the other Christian groups, it's a minority. God will just have to take care of the salvation matter. Obviously, it's in better hands that way.

Rather, the Church is to proclaim the Good News that God loves and offers salvation to all people. The Church has the mission to spread the word that this love of God is so great that God sent the Son, Jesus. That Good News, unfortunately, is still *news* to millions of people two thousand years after Jesus' coming.

The Church I believe in is a listening people, a people who, first of all, listen to Jesus. The Church I believe in listens to hear God's word also in the quiet of a time of prayer, in the events of our lives, in the needs of others, and in the signs of the times. And when we listen, we are called to respond.

The Church I believe in is called to be a community of love. We are a people who have accepted Jesus, who accept His primary teaching that God is a loving God. We believe that He loves us and that we ought to love one another. We are to carry on the teaching of Jesus, the perfect teacher, who teaches us not only in words but also in action. And He says, "Follow me." We are to love as He loves. I believe that if we who are the Church learn to love as Jesus loves, we will be transforming our world and bringing about the kingdom. The kingdom is already among us, Jesus says. But it has not yet fully come to be. In the Preface for the Feast of Christ the King we say of the kingdom:

> an eternal and universal kingdom
> a kingdom of truth and life
> a kingdom of holiness and grace
> a kingdom of justice, love and peace.

Clearly, we have a way to go to bring God's kingdom to perfection, and that is what the Church I believe in is really for.

The Church I believe in is also a remembering people. At the Last Supper, when Jesus transformed the bread and wine into His Body given and His Blood poured out, He said we should continue to do this to remember Him. And so we do, and we remember His death and resurrection in other sacraments, too. The Church I believe in is a sacramental Church.

The Church I believe in is a servant Church, dedicated to the service of all people but first of all to the poor and powerless. This is called the preferential option for the poor.

So you see, my friends, the Church I believe in is an unfinished work. It has had and continues to have some seemingly unrepentant scoundrels among its members. It has also had saints, both canonized and unofficial. In our day, it has had a laywoman, Dorothy Day, who served the poor and worked and suffered for peace. It has produced a Pope, John XXIII, who responded to the Spirit and the needs of the Church in the modern world. It has inspired a nun, Mother Teresa, to live among the poorest of the poor and devote herself to the care of the dying among them. In Oscar Romero, it has had an archbishop who identified with the oppressed and who died like a martyr for their cause.

This, my friends, is the Church I believe in. I hope that we are more the already than we are the not yet. More the holy than the sinful. More the loving than the unloving. I hope and pray, that you and I will want always to be a part of it, its celebrations and its works.

Peace!

Father Ed

QUESTIONS FOR REFLECTION AND DISCUSSION

1. When you think of the Church, what image comes to mind? Why do you think of the Church that way?
2. The first image of the Church that comes to mind may not be the way you would like to think of the Church. What is your preferred image? Why?
3. What changes would you like to see in the Church? What would you not want to change?

6

THE SACRAMENTS I BELIEVE IN

Dear Friends,

Many things have changed in the Church in the years I
have been a priest. All of us have been touched by the
changes--priests more than anyone else. This is especially
true in the celebration of the sacraments. We now use our
own language, and we have different ceremonies. There are
other changes, too, that are not so obvious but are more
profound, and these are in the way we understand the sacraments. I'd like to tell you a little about the sacraments I
believe in.

You probably remember the catechism definition that
says sacraments are signs. The catechism is speaking about
the seven sacraments, but it is important for us to realize
there are other sacraments. These, too, are signs. They are
sometimes things, sometimes places, even times. And sometimes they are actions.

In this understanding of sacrament, the beauty of nature
can be a sacrament. A thickly wooded area where the sunlight
only peeks through, a lake with waves gently splashing
against a stone retaining wall, a flock of honking geese flying
in V formation--all can speak to us of God the Creator and can
lead us to prayer and a deeper relationship with God. Morning and night can be sacraments because they seem to be
natural times to think of God and to pray. When we speak of
these things--nature, special times and places, even relation-

34

ships like friendship--as sacraments, we are embracing what is called the sacramental principle. This recognizes that God is present in all of creation, and all creation can speak to us of God. All we need are the eyes to see, the ears to hear, and the heart to respond.

But the sacraments I want most of all to write about are those seven that are at the center of the Church's life and have always been so.

There are sacraments I do not believe in. For example, I believe that they come to us from Christ, but I do not believe that at some time before His Ascension Jesus sat the twelve apostles down and said something to this effect: "Now, in this Church I am founding, there will be seven sacraments. These are their names, and this is how you will administer them."

I do not believe in sacraments which are to be thought of as concrete "things" so that we "receive" them and, in doing so, gain many graces. I do not believe in sacraments that work like magic: If the priest says the right words and makes the correct gestures, "it" happens. I do not believe in sacraments which are only or primarily for the individual, even if it is that person's special occasion, like a wedding. Even the sacrament of Penance, seemingly so individual and personal, is a restoring of a sinner to the community, like the lost sheep brought back to the flock. I am happy that the name *Rite of Reconciliation* expresses the communal and relational nature of the sacrament.

The sacraments I believe in are actions, and they are, first of all, the actions of Christ in His Church. Christ Himself is the first sacrament, the living and acting sign of God's presence in our world. After Christ's resurrection and ascension, when He was no longer visible, He was no longer a sign in the same sense. The Church, then, the body of Christ, came to see itself as the sacrament of God's loving presence among people. The sacraments I believe in are community signs, the Christian community's, with community understanding. They are actions which speak the understanding and faith of the community.

The world outside of the Church also has such signs; *secular sacraments* we can call them. Saluting the flag is a sign which speaks to all of us, but it is easy to understand that it will speak more movingly to a veteran who has served in battle. Joining a group of citizens in saluting the flag is an expression of patriotism, of loyalty to one's country. This sacramental action not only expresses but also fosters patriotism. A handshake, too, is a kind of sacramental action; it is a sign of a relationship, and, in the act of shaking hands, the relationship is strengthened. Even more so, the expressions of love between husband and wife are sacramental signs. They express their love, and in these actions, their love is fostered and deepened.

Places, too, can be sacraments, not simply as places but because of their history, what people did or experienced there. In this way, the desert was a sacrament for the Jews. For forty years they had wandered in that hot and hostile wasteland. It was a place of purification, and it was where they entered into covenant with Yahweh. Yahweh would be their God and they would be Yahweh's people. In later times, when Yahweh's people fell into idolatry, the prophets would call them back to the desert--not to the place but to the conversion they had experienced there and to a renewal of the covenant relationship they had begun with Yahweh there.

Families, also, often have symbols or in-house signs which recall events in their shared life. These can be gestures, meals on special occasions, and even nicknames. These symbols have power, and the more those who are participating understand the symbols and have shared the experience of these special events, the more these signs deepen the relationships and sense of belonging in the family.

The sacraments I believe in, my friends, are likewise the signs and symbols of a family, the family of God which we call the Church. They recall and celebrate what God has done for us in Christ. The more we know of our faith community's history and the more we ourselves share that history by living that faith, the more these signs speak to us, and the more effectively Christ can act in us. This is what we mean when we say that sacraments give grace. And that is why in every celebration of a sacrament there is a Liturgy of the Word. Here something of our history as God's people is retold and we are encouraged to continue in that ongoing story of God among people.

Some of that history is ancient, going back to the times of the Hebrew Scriptures, centuries before the birth of Jesus. For example, consider the sacrament of Baptism. For many years, I thought of this sacrament primarily in terms of removing original sin. In my thinking, the pouring of the water was the sacramental sign of washing away that sin.

If we know the history of the Jews, which is also our history, we can see that there is much more to the sign of this sacrament. The Jews as a people cherish memories of a number of experiences with water. Two of these are the most vivid. These memories have a powerful, formative influence on their community-religious life. Both of these are important to our understanding of Baptism. One is the memory of the deluge in Noah's time. In this flood, water was a frightening instrument of God's power and of destruction. The other memory is of an event on their journey through the desert. When they feared that they were perishing for lack of water, they cried out to God. God heard them and directed Moses to strike a rock, and an abundance of fresh, life-saving water gushed forth! At one time, water was an instrument of death; at the other, it was a means of saving their lives.

When the Church, in its earliest days, developed its baptismal ceremonies, it had in mind these life and death experiences of God's people. It shaped a ritual in which the person about to be baptized stepped down into the water, rejected Satan and sin, accepted Jesus and the Church, and was baptized. The newly baptized then emerged from the water and put on a new white robe. In word and action: death and new life! Death to sin, new life in Christ.

So, the sacraments I believe in are celebrations of a family, the family of God--powerful, grace-filled celebrations. I don't think they should ever be thought of in individualistic terms. Baptism, for instance, does not bring us as individuals into a relationship with God. We have that from the beginning of our life. What Baptism does is this: It brings us into a new relationship with God as Father because we have been reborn into Christ, God's only Son. Since God becomes our

Father in a special way in Baptism, we become members of a family that includes all of God's children. This is the Church. All the sacraments I believe in are celebrations of this family of God, and all of them enrich this family's life.

The other sacraments I believe in intensify our relationship with Christ, plunge us more deeply into the dynamism of His dying and rising. In Christ, that process is complete; in us, it continues until our final and definitive dying, when our obituary appears in the paper. This lifelong process of dying to whatever is sinful and rising to a life more like Christ's is, I believe, the necessary prelude to our final and definitive rising in Christ to full and never-ending life with Him, the Father and the Spirit in heaven.

So, the sacraments I believe in are actions in which the God of heaven and earth, the Creator and Ruler of the universe, meets us in ways that we can hear and see and feel--in ways that fit our body-spirit nature. Some years ago, I heard a talk by a psychologist. In the course of his talk, he told this story. As he was tending an elderly woman who was very ill, a priest came to anoint her. When he had completed the prayers and anointing, the priest bent down and tenderly kissed the woman on her forehead. The psychologist fairly shouted, "That should be written into the rubrics!" I agree. The sacraments I believe in, all of them, are God bending down to us in Christ, forgiving and embracing us, nourishing and strengthening us, drawing us always closer in God's love.

Peace!

Father Ed

QUESTIONS FOR REFLECTION OR DISCUSSION

1. Did my sharing my beliefs about the sacraments offer you a new understanding of the sacraments? If it did, in what way?
2. Sacraments are sign-actions, like saluting the flag, shaking hands. Reflect on the fact that the more we understand the signs, the greater the impact they have on us.
3. Sacraments are community actions. Discuss the advantages and disadvantages of Baptisms at Sunday Mass and of Communal Penance Services.

7

THE EUCHARIST I BELIEVE IN

Dear Friends,

I must confess that for quite a while I have wanted to write about the Eucharist I believe in. There may be many reasons why I haven't done so, but one I am sure of: I just haven't been able to focus on what I want to say. The Eucharist means so much--how do I write about it?

We say that it is the greatest sacrament, that it is the heart of our Catholic life. Vatican II, I recall, speaks of the Eucharist as the source and summit of Christian life and action. (See *The Constitution on the Sacred Liturgy*, article 10.) Source and summit--that says so much. And Pope John XXIII, when asked where he drew his strength and inspiration from, said simply: The Book and the Cup. The Eucharist. Like so many things in our faith, it is a mystery, a reality too rich for us to understand, too marvelous for us to put into adequate words, too good, it seems, to be true--and yet true it is!

The Eucharist I believe in is good news and hard sayings. It is consolation and challenge. It is memorial and food for our journey through life.

When we face something that is too much for us, we tend to pick it apart, isolate some elements we think we can deal with and talk about them. This became evident, for instance, after the Second Vatican Council and the changes it brought.

Rather than reflect on the meaning of the Eucharist as a whole, some people focused on little things. I recall, for example, an occasion in the early 1970s when I was asked by a parish society to speak in response to questions submitted in writing by its members. One of the questions was, "Why doesn't our priest wear the black robe anymore when he says Mass?" I must confess that I was tempted to say that the question itself had a number of mistakes, but I refrained and tried to give them an overview of the theology of Vatican II and the Eucharist and then answer their particular questions.

Even so, I was not satisfied when I finished, and I offered them a number of questions I wish they had asked. One of these was, "In view of all of the changes going on in the Church, in the world, and in family life in particular, how can Catholic parents pass on their faith and values to their children?" The question is as relevant today as it was at that time. (Incidentally, they asked me to come back to answer the questions I had raised.)

At the heart of the answer to the question I suggested is the Eucharist, the source and summit of Christian life. But I'm sure you realize that the Eucharist I believe in involves much more than the the priest's wearing a cassock, much more than simply going to Church when the priest "says" Mass. The Eucharist I believe in is not something the priest says; it is not even something the priest does, although that is closer. The Eucharist is, first of all, the action of Christ. Christ does it in all the members of His body, lay women and men and priests together. If we understand this, then we can see that a better question from that parish group might have been, "How can we participate more fully in the Eucharist?"

The Eucharist I believe in usually takes place in the parish community but it begins at home, at work, in school. It begins with our everyday lives and actions. The Eucharist I believe in is a celebration of who we are as Christians. When we sing that the world will know we are Christians by our love, it means not only in Church but at our office, in the kitchen, on the assembly line, at the computer terminal. Many years ago, in a little magazine entitled *Integrity*, there was a quatrain that struck me. The original began "Mr.

Business" and was written in the past tense. I have changed that to "Sunday Catholics" and put it into the present tense:

> Sunday Catholics go to Mass.
> They never miss a Sunday.
> Sunday Catholics go to hell
> For what they do on Monday.

Although I do not like the emphasis on hell, the connection between what we do all week and our Sunday Eucharist is a valid one.

The Eucharist I believe in is a family celebration for the family of God. When families get together to celebrate, there usually is much happy talk, recounting of shared memories and, of course, a meal. In the telling of family stories, customs and values are passed on to younger members. In the eating of the meal, family bonds are strengthened. In much the same way, the Eucharist means gathering the family, telling *the* story, and sharing the bread and the wine. The story, the happy talk, is the Good News, remembering God's saving actions all through history on our behalf. The meal of bread and wine is the Body and Blood of the Lord.

Gathering the family. We come from many places, but we are one family, born from above as sons and daughters in our Baptism into Christ. Our gathering at Eucharist, as our gathering for our natural family celebrations, is more than physical, bodily presence. In the Eucharist I believe in we come together body and spirit, with a common history and with shared values. That body-spirit oneness should be shown. This is why in many parishes the priest and other ministers are at the door to welcome all as they enter. I like what one priest said: The test of parish hospitality is whether you can get into the gathering without being touched.

When families gather and family events are remembered and retold, those events almost seem to come alive in the telling. In the Eucharist I believe in, in the Scripture readings, the story of our faith family, the events become present in a very real way. Jesus, I believe, is present in His word. In the Eucharist, Jesus is once again inviting sinners, the

41

physically, emotionally, and spiritually crippled. Once again, Jesus the healer, the consoler, is present and active among His people. Once again, Jesus is instructing and challenging us to follow Him, even to Calvary.

...what all of us do all week is what we bring to Eucharist.

All words, we know, have power. And, in a sense, the words of people in positions of authority have special effectiveness. At the words of earth's rulers, bridges and buildings go up and people's heads come off. Think, then, of God's word! We say it is sacramental: It does the work God sends it to do. This part of the Eucharist I believe in, the Liturgy of the Word--just like the storytelling in family celebrations--is nourishing and strengthening and is as essential to the celebration as the meal is.

When families gather for special occasions, sometimes the members bring not only memories to share but also dishes of food as part of the meal. These home-prepared offerings are symbolic. They are signs of the oneness of the family. In the Eucharist, too, all of us bring a gift, and that gift is ourselves. We place ourselves on the altar-table, not physically of course, but in intention, in our free will, and so, in all we willingly do. And we do it in symbol, in the bringing of the bread and wine, fruits of God's good earth and the work of human hands.

In the summer of 1947 I had an extraordinary experience. It dramatized that what all of us do all week is what we bring to the Eucharist. A number of us seminarians participated in the closing Mass of the International Jocists' (Young Christian Workers) Study Week in Montreal. It was an outdoor Mass and Canon Cardijn (later Cardinal Cardijn, although he never became a bishop) preached at great length in both English and French. When this founder of the Jocists finished, workers in procession filed in carrying pre-cut lumber and fashioned the altar. Women followed and "set the table" with the altar cloths, chalice, and candlesticks. Finally, the bread and wine were presented. This was 1947, more than a decade before Vatican II was even thought of!

And then the eating of the meal. The Eucharistic meal, just as the Eucharistic Word, is something like our family meal, but also so much more. It is a meal that remembers and makes present the death and resurrection of our Lord. It is a meal in which time and space dissolve and what Jesus did on that first Holy Thursday, Good Friday, and Easter Sunday becomes present and active in this time and place, in us! At the Last Supper, Jesus gathered His disciples, the ones who had become His family. At the end of the meal, He brought together all of His life--a life that included and summed up all the history of His people, a life that anticipated His total gift of Himself to the Father in His death and resurrection--and presented it to His disciples and us under the appearance of bread and wine.

When Jesus says, "This is my body," He is speaking as a Jew. *Body* in that culture means "me." *Blood* means "life." In the Eucharist I believe in, Jesus offers us Himself and His entire life--a life that has assumed, relived, purified, and perfected the life of His people. When we accept His person and His life, unite with them in the intimate union of Communion, we make them ours. When we become one with Christ, we become one with all who are one with Christ--the unemployed young man in the ghetto, the lonely grandmother in a nursing home, the impoverished people in developing countries.

Jesus calls this cup of wine "the new covenant in my blood." Covenants were ancient forms of agreement, something like our contracts, but much more personal. Jesus is bringing the old covenant to its fulfillment. It was entered into on Mount Sinai and was remembered and renewed annually in the Passover Meal. In this covenant agreement with the Jewish people, God would be their God and the people said they would be God's people. You and I enter into the new covenant in Baptism. We renew it in the Body and Blood of Christ in every Eucharist. In this covenant there is no fine print: Christ's love for us is unconditional. It calls for unconditional love in return.

All this history and all this action is condensed, compressed into one hour. It all passes so quickly, and it is more than we can be conscious of at every Eucharist. What we can do is try to come to the realization that the Eucharist is always. In includes all of our life just as it includes all of Christ's life. The Eucharist I believe in is the gift of ourselves, our commitment to God's plan, the building of the kingdom along with Christ. And, finally, the Eucharist I believe in is the source of all our strength.

Eucharistic peace!

Father Ed

QUESTIONS FOR REFLECTION AND DISCUSSION

1. In what ways can good family celebrations enhance our appreciation of the Eucharist?
2. How can the Eucharistic celebration in your parish resemble a family meal? How can this resemblance be strengthened?

8

THE MARY I BELIEVE IN

Dear Friends,

I have often been asked what I believe about Mary. In telling you what I believe, I will try to picture Mary in a realistic way, in a human way that will help you relate to her, because the Mary I believe in can indeed be a model for every contemporary follower of Christ. Mary is what each of us is called to become.

If I am to tell you about the Mary I believe in, I need to tell you something of my personal history in relation to Mary. When I was in the seminary, we had a number of student groups devoted to special interests. Some seminarians gathered to study and discuss the lay apostolate; others, the Catholic labor movement; still others, the liturgy. There was also a Marian group. I know that Marian groups have been generous in their service in parishes in this country. I know, too, that their work in times of persecution in some other countries has been truly heroic. Even so, there was something about this group, or perhaps I should rather say, about some of the members of this group, that turned me and some of my friends off. They seemed, for instance, to give the impression that if you were not in their group, you did not love Mary. Unfortunately, the difficulty I had with some of their attitudes carried over, at least to some extent, into my relationship with Mary herself.

I was ordained in 1948. It was a time of great interest in
Mary. Perpetual Help Devotions were popular in most parishes; some had devotions to Our Lady of the Miraculous
Medal, the Sorrowful Mother, and others. Block Rosaries were
organized in many parishes. Fatima was being discovered in
our country. And in 1950, Pope Pius XII proclaimed that
Mary, at the end of her life, was assumed body and soul into
heaven.

Much of what went on in these devotions and move-
ments surely was good, and much, I believe, was an expression of genuine faith. I think, further, that these things filled
a need for some people, especially because the celebrations of
the liturgy at that time were frequently remote and somewhat
inaccessible.

Although it was a heady time of devotion to Mary, I'm
afraid not all of this was good theology and healthy spirituality. For example, it was in 1950, the same year that Pope Pius
XII proclaimed the doctrine of the assumption, that Mary Ann
Van Hoof in Necedah, Wisconsin, was claiming appearances of
Mary with messages for all, and thousands of pilgrims were
traveling to that little town to see and hear her. More than a
hundred miles from Necedah, in the parish I was serving, a
woman called the rectory to report that she had seen the sun
spinning in the sky. She was convinced that this was proof of
the claims of Mrs. Van Hoof.

In addition, there were exaggerated claims and expectations concerning Mary and her role in our ongoing redemption
by Jesus. So, it was a mixed picture, and I think you can
understand, there was much in all this that I could not
believe.

I do not believe, for instance, that we go to Jesus through
Mary. I believe it is the other way around. I do not believe
that we have to go to Mary to be heard or that she will change
the mind of Jesus and get Him to help us. I do not believe, as
the story goes, that after our death, if Jesus closes the door of
heaven to us, Mary will open a window to let us in. I do not
believe that every apparent miracle in nature is a sign vali-
dating a claim of an appearance of our Blessed Mother. I am
afraid that all of these things, taken together, contributed to a

negative feeling and attitude on my part toward Mary herself and I did not like that. I decided that prayer and reflection on the Scriptures should be my approach to correcting my problem. I can now tell you about the Mary I have come to believe in.

When we read the Scriptures, we see that there are not many words there devoted to Mary, but what is there tells us so much. The picture of Mary that emerges is of a person who is quiet, unassuming, totally dedicated to God's will, extraordinarily strong and outgoing in her love and concern for others.

The Mary I believe in is totally dedicated to God's will. When the angel Gabriel appears to her to tell her she has been chosen to be the mother of the Redeemer, Mary's response is simple and direct: "Behold, I am the handmaid of the Lord. May it be done to me according to your word" (Luke 1:38). The Gospel account is stark in its simplicity, and it is probably impossible for us to appreciate what a shock this encounter was to the young Mary. It was an invitation to accept an honor, to be sure, but think of the responsibility! And think of the change it brings to her life's plans. And Mary says in effect, simply and directly: Whatever God wants, I want.

This openness and response of Mary to God's will is beautifully and poetically expressed in Caryll Houselander's book *The Reed of God.* The idea is that a reed must be emptied out to become a musical instrument. Mary became the reed of God, allowing God's tune to be played through her.

I think all of us have moments when we feel we can say something like that, but if we are honest, we have to admit that we often slip back into our usual way of life--a life much less than totally dedicated. Mary, however, follows through. When she says, "What God wants, I want," it is her autobiography in miniature. This is her life.

There is another passage in Scripture about Mary, not directly related to this but which I associate with it. It is the simple directive Mary gives to the waiters at the wedding at Cana: "Do whatever he tells you" (John 2:5). It seems to me to flow so naturally from Mary's lips because that is what she is doing in the whole of her own life. In a sense, she is saying, "Do as I do."

Sometime later, Jesus is asked by one of His disciples: "Teach us to pray..." (Luke 11:1). In response, Jesus gives them and us the Our Father. In this prayer, we say, "Thy kingdom come, Thy will be done." This is an example of Hebraic parallelism. The two phrases mean the same thing. The kingdom will come when enough people say and mean, "Whatever God wants, I want." The repetition in the prayer is a way of expressing its importance. The Scriptures show us that even before Jesus gives us this prayer, Mary has embraced it and made it her way of life.

The kingdom will come when enough people say and mean, "Whatever God wants, I want."

The Mary I believe in is concerned about others. Let us look at the Annunciation again. After the angel leaves her, Mary, now pregnant with the Redeemer of the world, sets off to the hill country to help her cousin Elizabeth, who is also expecting a child. He will be known as John the Baptist. Jesus will later say that He Himself has come not to be served but to serve. Mary, who has just been given the greatest dignity of any human person, is here exemplifying that kind of concern and dedication to service.

When Mary arrives at Elizabeth's home, Elizabeth exclaims, "Most blessed are you among women and blessed is the fruit of your womb" (Luke 1:42). Mary's response is the Magnificat. In this prayer, she briefly praises God for what God has done for her and then turns to what God has done for the lowly, the poor, and the hungry. The Mary I believe in is always thinking of others.

Now, let me come back to the wedding at Cana. Frequently it is used as an example of the power of Mary's intercession, and I have no quarrel with that. My focus here, however, is on how it shows Mary's concern for others, her willingness to be involved. You remember the story, I am sure. The young couple is in danger of running out of wine at their reception. In that culture, this would be a terrible embarrassment. In the Gospel story, no one comes to Mary to ask her to intercede with Jesus for them--Mary takes the initiative and does so confidently and successfully.

There is something else here that strikes me. The wedding at Cana is at the beginning of the public life of Jesus, and Mary is here with her Son. Then on the way to Calvary and at the crucifixion, the end of His public life, Mary is again with Him. I think this is a way of saying that, even though she is not mentioned frequently throughout the Gospel, Mary is with Jesus all through His public life, even to its cruel and tragic end on the cross. No matter how we wish to paint the picture of our redemption by Jesus, Mary has to be in that picture. The Mary I believe in is a strong and faithful person.

The Mary I believe in is a fully human woman and mother. There is a Bible story that seems to me to show her human qualities. It is the finding of Jesus in the Temple when He was twelve years old. Mary, Joseph, and Jesus traveled from Galilee in the North to Jerusalem in the South. It was a difficult journey, by foot or donkey. There was also constant danger from bandits. For protection, families traveled in groups. During the day, the men were together, the women and children in another section of the caravan. As a boy of twelve, Jesus could have been with either the men or the women. In the evening, the travelers gathered as families, and it was at this time that they discovered that Jesus was not with either group. Perhaps only a parent can appreciate the panic that filled the hearts of Mary and Joseph. It was another long day's journey back to Jerusalem and I am sure it seemed much longer this time. Finally, on the third day, physically and emotionally exhausted, Mary and Joseph found Jesus in the Temple. When Mary asked Him, "Why have you done so to us?" I sense not only tremendous relief, but also more than a hint of impatience in her voice. I think it was real impatience.

Let me conclude, my friends, with a final thought about

the Mary I believe in. Do you remember the time Jesus said to Peter, "Get behind me, Satan?" The use of the name, Satan, for Peter, catches our attention. It sounds frightening. Actually, the role of Satan is to be a "stumbling block" and Peter is being a stumbling block to Jesus because he is objecting to the prediction Jesus has just made of His passion and death. What I am especially interested in here is the expression, "Get behind me." Although it seems to be a kind of rejection of Peter, I think it can also mean something quite different. I think it can mean "to get behind" in the sense of "to follow." Jesus is telling Peter that he is not thinking like a follower of Jesus. He is telling Peter to get back in His following, to think like a disciple again. That call of Jesus to Peter is a call of Jesus to each one of us--even when following includes difficult decisions. The Mary I believe in is such a disciple, consistent in her faithfulness, totally dedicated, and always concerned about others. She is what we are to become.

Peace!

Father Ed

QUESTIONS FOR REFLECTION OR DISCUSSION

1. Do you agree that Mary can be a model for contemporary Christians? If yes, in what way? If not, why not?
2. What event in the life of Mary mentioned in the Scriptures is your favorite? Why?

9

THE COMMANDMENTS
I BELIEVE IN

Dear Friends,

I know that the subject of the Commandments or laws
bothers some people. It raises images of a repressive God.
Some find that the Commandments do not help them think of
a God who creates us and loves us. For these people, the
Commandments cloud over the picture of the God who gives
us freedom. The Commandments get in the way of their
seeing the God who offers us forgiveness when we misuse that
freedom. I don't think it has to be that way.

There are commandments I don't believe in. Commandments that are made for God. Commandments that are
designed to inhibit us from healthy growth. Commandments
that make us unhappy. I don't believe in commandments
which extend to minor matters, such as an impatient word or
a passing sexual thought, in such a way that these deserve
severe punishment.

There are commandments, too, that I do believe in. Look
at the Ten Commandments. They have been part of our
tradition in the Church and in our Jewish origins for three
thousand years. Symbols that are an important part of
people's lives for that long are significant and sacred. But that
does not mean that I believe everything every preacher or

51

teacher that you and I have had has said about them.

The Commandments that I believe in are the same Commandments I learned in grade school. But it was a long time later that I learned what I now think is the most important thing about them. It has to do with the setting in which they were given to us. God gave the Commandments to Moses in a covenant setting. I am sure you remember how Moses led the Israelites out of Egypt. When they were safely out of reach of the Egyptian army, God appeared to Moses and recalled all that God had done for the people: God had freed them from slavery, fed them on their journey through the desert, and borne them up on eagle's wings.

The Ten Commandments...are for our benefit, not for God's. God does not need our obedience.

Eagles nest in very high places. I have been told that when the young are ready to fly, the mother eagle nudges one of them out of the nest and it falls. Instinctively the young bird begins to fly and the mother stays close. When the young one becomes tired, the mother swoops down and, with wings outstretched, glides beneath her offspring and catches it on top of her wing. She takes it to a perch to rest and then repeats the process.

God brought the people out of Egypt on eagle's wings. Always close by, ready to help when they could not make it on their own. Then God offered them a covenant. God offered to enter into a lasting relationship with them. They would be special to God and God to them. When Moses told this to the people, they said, "Everything the Lord has said, we will do." God then took Moses to the top of Mount Sinai and gave him the Ten Commandments. The first one is not only first in numerical order; it is first in importance. I'm afraid, however, we do not usually say it with the correct emphasis. We need to remember that this is in a covenant setting. This commandment is the expression of a relationship. The commandment reads, "I am the Lord, *your* God. You shall not have other gods besides me."

Keeping these Commandments is to be our way of saying that we accept God, that God is indeed *our* God, that we are God's people. Keeping the Commandments is a way of saying that God is special to us and we want to be special to God.

There is another important thing about the Commandments that I did not learn until long after I had memorized them. When we, in our society, with our traditions, hear the words *commandments* or *laws*, they can come across as harsh and rigid. We tend to think of religious commandments as though they were like our civil laws, with police, law courts, and jails. The Ten Commandments I believe in are not like that. The word used in the Bible for commandments means "instructions" or simply "words." These are God's words to us, they are God's instructions, and they are for our benefit, not for God's. God does not need our obedience.

When we think of laws in our way, like civil laws, we often want to rebel. We do not like someone telling us what we may or may not do, what we must do. I remember telling a friend of mine about a problem someone was having with a private drive at his lake cottage. People kept coming in and then having difficulty because there was not adequate room for turning around except right at the house. My friend is a salesman and has keen insights into psychology. He asked what kind of a sign marked the entrance to the private drive. I said it was the standard sign: *Private Road, Keep Out.* My friend said, "Tell the owner to get a sign that reads: *Dead End, No Turnaround.* In this way, people will understand that keeping out is for their own good."

I have done something like this with children in school, too. I have asked them which commandment they would drop if they had the choice. Often it will be the Fourth Commandment, about obeying their parents. Then I explain that the commandment really includes two things: They are to obey their parents, yes, and their parents are to provide for them and take care of them. Do they want to give that up? I also point out that they probably will marry some day. If they become parents, would they then want that commandment eliminated? Sometimes some of them mention the Seventh Commandment, about stealing. They think it would be neat if they could take whatever they want. But then they realize that others could take their things, too. They come to appreciate that the Commandments are really for us, for our good. They are necessary for order and peace in our society.

The Commandments I believe in are a response, a people's response to their experience of God. The Israelites experienced God not as harsh or capricious. They experienced God as gracious, loving, and caring. Their obedience to the law was born of gratitude for God's goodness to them. To help them keep in mind all that God had done, they had special feasts and rituals to celebrate God's works.

We have all had the experience of having to do without something and then coming to a renewed appreciation of it when we have it again. This is true of the Israelites who, for a long time, were nomads, without land of their own. When they came to the land that God gave them and were able to grow their food, they established the custom of taking the firstfruits of their harvest to the priest. Here they recited a formula which began, "My father was a wandering Aramean...." It went on to recount how this landless ancestor, Abraham, was called by God, how his descendants were delivered from slavery in Egypt, how God brought them to this land of milk and honey. In thankfulness for all this, they were responding by bringing these gifts as a sign that they were God's covenanted people and would keep God's Commandments.

For the faithful Jew, the Commandments are not a burden but a blessing. They are an expression of a deep and mutually caring relationship between God and the person. It is commandments like these that I believe in.

Many of us will remember seeing pictures of Moses with the two tablets of stone on which God had carved the Ten Commandments. In the catechism I used--I can still remember this!--they had three numbers on the first tablet and the remaining seven on the second. This is not because the first three are so lengthy. It is because the first three refer directly to God and the other seven to what God instructs us to do in relationship with one another. Actually, the Commandments are not numbered in the Bible, and some religious traditions divide them differently. For them, the first three in our list are divided into four. Then, in the latter half, they combine two of ours into one. In this division, four refer to God and the last six to our neighbor. Only the numbering is different; the content is the same.

The way the Commandments are numbered is not important, but the fact that they are divided into two sets of relationships is. You may remember the occasion when Jesus was asked which is the greatest commandment in the law. The setting is this: It is after He has come into Jerusalem on the first Palm Sunday. The people had waved palm branches before Him and sung His praises. They had placed their cloaks on the path Jesus was traveling. After this popular demonstration in His honor, Jesus' enemies called a meeting to plot His destruction. They decided to approach Him with a series of trick questions, hoping to discredit Him in the minds of the people. One of these questions was about the law. The Gospel says that a lawyer, in an attempt to trip Him up, asked Him, "Teacher, which commandment of the law is the greatest?" (Matthew 22:36).

The Jewish law contained 613 prescriptions. It was a kind of sport among the lawyers to debate which was the most important. Jesus was not interested in their games, but He immediately responded, "You shall love the Lord, your God, with all your heart, with all your soul, and with all your mind. This is the greatest and the first commandment." Then Jesus went beyond answering the question. "The second," Jesus said, "is like it: You shall love your neighbor as yourself. The whole law and the prophets depend on these two command-ments" (Matthew 22:37:40).

What Jesus is saying here is amazing. He is saying that all that God has revealed as important in our relationships with God and with one another is contained in these two laws. If we love God this way, we will honor God. If we love our neighbors as ourselves, we will respect them and all that is theirs. But Jesus went further. At the Last Supper, He inaugurated a new covenant with its own commandment: We are to love one another as He, Jesus, loves us. Jesus tells us that love fulfills the law.

Some people, I know, are afraid that teaching that all the Commandments are contained in the one law of love is a way of weakening the demands of the Christian life. I do not think so. Love actually makes greater demands than the letter of the law. Look at the story of the good Samaritan. A priest and a Levite saw the man who had been beaten and robbed lying in the ditch, and they passed by. They did not beat him, rob him, or push him deeper into the ditch. They did not break any of the Ten Commandments. But they did not fulfill the commandment of love. The commandment of love asks more of us. And we are never finished with this commandment: We always continue to owe love.

These, my friends, are the Commandments I believe in. They are Commandments that are for our good, Commandments that express our relationship with God and with each other. Commandments that are summed up in love. I hope that you and I can always see them not as a burden but as a blessing.

Peace!

Father Ed

QUESTIONS FOR DISCUSSION OR REFLECTION

1. If we see the Commandments in the context of our relationship with God, is it easier to accept them? Discuss.
2. Think of how the commandment of love might apply to us in relationship to:

- *the poor in the developing countries*
- *minority people in our inner cities*
- *immigrants to our country*
- *care for the environment*

10

THE PRAYER I BELIEVE IN

Dear Friends,

People often tell me that they wish they could pray better. That is a wholesome wish. You may recall that the apostles once asked Jesus, "Lord, teach us to pray." That request was itself a prayer. And it is a prayer that has been echoed in the hearts and words of men and women throughout the centuries.

There is a kind of prayer that I don't believe in. I don't believe in prayer which is a way of bargaining with God; for example, "God, if you will give me this, I will go to Mass every day for a month." And the prayer which is like a form of magic. I see this when people ask me, "Father, do you know a good prayer for someone with cancer?" or "...to get someone back to church?" This makes it sound as if God's gift can be had only by saying the right words. Obviously, I don't believe in the prayers which used to circulate more often years ago but which still appear occasionally today. These are chain prayers. If you say this special prayer formula for a certain number of days, and make and give out the right number of copies, you will have great good fortune. And, the letter warns, if you break the chain, you will suffer dire consequences. I am sure that many of the people who spread these formulas and letters are good people. I am sure, too, that God loves them, but I do not believe in those kinds of prayers.

The prayer I believe in is an expression of faith and an act of religion. Religion, I believe, is relationships. God is revealed in relationships. God relates as friend to Adam and Eve in the Garden of Paradise. The prophet Hosea speaks of God as a spouse and faithful lover. Jesus pictures God as a father, a loving and forgiving father. The prophet Isaiah compares God to a mother and says that even if a mother should forget the infant nursing at her breast, God will not forget us. In response to His apostles' request to teach them to pray, Jesus gives them the Our Father. All of these speak of relationships between God and us. The prayer that Jesus gives us is both a formula for prayer and a pattern for prayers of our own.

The kind of prayer I believe in depends on the kind of God I believe in, because the prayer I believe in is a way of being with God. It is a way of listening and talking, of being loved and loving, a way of being possessed and possessing. It is a way of thinking about and doing for. I recently read something about prayer of this kind that I like very much. It was written by Monsignor George Niederauer in the 1991 summer issue of *Church* magazine: "The American Catholic struggle to pray can be called 'A Tale of Two Benches.' The two benches are the bus bench and the park bench. I go to the bus bench pragmatically....I go to the park bench just to go to the park bench....Nothing is produced; nothing gets done....Prayer...is the quintessential park bench activity."

Prayer is always a gift. It is always God who initiates prayer.

The prayer I believe in is a way of being with God. Prayer is always a gift. It is always God who initiates prayer, and it is also God who graces us with the desire to pray. God acts and we respond. In the motion picture *Therese*, Sister Therese of Lisieux is called "Sister Amen." We, in prayer, are to be amens to the action of God.

The prayer I believe in is usually quite ordinary. It can be a quick "Thank you" to God for another day or for something good that just happened or for something that I only now have become aware of. It can be a short intercession when I feel the need. It may be a quiet time when I can think and say what is in my heart.

The prayer I believe in has to look to other people, too, because the God I believe in says so. In the prayer Jesus gave us, we begin "Our Father," not "My Father." Jesus also tells us that if we are bringing our gift to the altar and there we remember that our brother or sister has anything against us, we are to leave our gift at the altar, go first to be reconciled, and then bring our gift. Only then can we worship God. And St. John tells us that if we do not love a brother or sister we have seen, we cannot love God, whom we have not seen. And further, St. John writes that if we say we love God but hate a brother or sister, we are liars. (See 1 John 4:20.)

The prayer I believe in must first of all be honest. If I, at a particular moment, feel weak or see my relationship with God as one of dependence, if I feel unable to meet my own or others' needs, if I don't know where to turn or what to do, then my prayer will be one of petition. It helps me when I remember that Jesus prayed that kind of prayer in the Garden of Olives: "My Father, if it is possible, let this cup pass me by. Still, let it be as you would have it, not as I." (See Matthew 26:41.)

If I know that I have been unfaithful or unloving in my relationship with God or those around me--in other words, that I have sinned--then, if my prayer is to be honest, it will have to be a prayer of sorrow. But this prayer of sorrow will not be an unhealthy, worrying kind because Jesus assures us there will be more joy in heaven over one repentant sinner than over ninety-nine righteous people who have no need to repent.

If I am feeling good and happy and I am enjoying the world or friends, or if I am thinking of Jesus and all He has done, I will want to pray the prayer of thanks. Jesus often turned to His Father and ours in this kind of prayer. And, in contrast, one of the sadder moments in the Gospels is the time that Jesus heals the ten lepers and only one comes back to thank Him. One can almost feel the disappointment in His voice as Jesus asks, "Ten were cleansed, were they not? Where are the other nine?" (Luke 17:17).

If I feel loved and want to love in return, then that will be the kind of prayer I will pray. The prayer I believe in, then, is an honest, human expression of my relationship with the God I believe in. But it is more than a mere expression. The prayer I believe in deepens that relationship. When people who are in love take time to share their thoughts and hopes, they grow in their love through that sharing. And so, when we pray, we not only express our love for God, we grow in it. The prayer I believe in is sacramental; it does things and it changes us.

There are books written on prayer. Some are theoretical books on what prayer is and the various kinds of prayer. There are also practical how-to books. What I want to do is offer some suggestions in the area of how to pray.

Pray from your own experience. Pray from the experience of the whole of your life. Just be with God and talk to God about your life, your needs, your hopes. You can talk about the good things and the bad things that have happened, about your joys and angers. Yes, you can tell God about your angers, but not only the angers. I think that is important. Learn to listen to what is going on inside of you, what the Spirit is doing in your life, and talk to God about it. Talk about what God has given you: your body, your mind, your special talents, family, and friends. Talk about the beautiful world, the freedom you enjoy.

Pray from the Scriptures. This is really another way of praying out of experience. The Scriptures are the experience of God's people, and in many ways those experiences are very much like our own. The psalms, for example, express just about every human mood and need. We can also take some other book of the Bible. The Gospels are probably the easiest for us. We can read and reflect and say to God whatever seems appropriate. Recently I stopped at a home when the person living there was not expecting me. It was after she had told me of her anger and frustration with someone. While she was out of the room, I noticed that her Bible was open, and when I looked at it, I saw that it was opened to the passage where Jesus tells us to love our enemies. If she was reflecting on that call of Jesus and speaking to Him about it, that would be a beautiful prayer. Even if she was not able to love that person perfectly at the time--we never do anything perfectly anyway--that would still be a beautiful prayer.

Pray out of familiar prayer formulas. You can use formulas to help you pray, but you should not be bound or restricted by them. Praying is the important thing, not the formula. You can take the words, "Give us this day our daily bread," or, "Forgive us our trespasses as we forgive those who trespass against us" and spend time with them with God. When I visit the very sick, who are sometimes too weak for many words, I often repeat the words, "Thy will be done on earth as it is in heaven." I tell them that this means that they want what God wants and that nothing is more important.

There's another group of formulas that you can use, sacramental texts. For instance, the baptismal promises can be a way of rededicating ourselves to the living of the Christ-life. The formulas for the pouring of the water and the anointing can re-enforce the sense of our dignity and worth before God.

Pray with your body. In some ways we, who have a Catholic background, are familiar with this. We are used to praying the Sign of the Cross, to genuflecting, to kneeling, to folding our hands. These are all forms of praying with the body, and we do them especially in the Liturgy. We can pray body-prayers when we are alone, also. We can use the ones we have learned, and we can make up our own body-prayers. They can be postures, something like some of the postures many people know from Yoga. They can be something as simple as sitting quietly and holding out open hands. Bowing or even just a loving look at a crucifix or a book of the Gospels can be a prayer. Body-prayers can be dance. This form of prayer is as ancient as the dance of King David before the Ark of the Covenant. Let your imagination create your body-prayers. Words can be added, but they are not always neces-

sary. Our bodies themselves can speak our relationship to
God.

Pray in song. It is often said that people in love like to
sing. Praying is an act of love, and the singing of prayers has
a long tradition. The psalms, for instance, were meant to be
sung. Most often when we sing our prayers, it is when we are
with others, at a meal, a discussion or prayer group, or above
all at the Eucharist. But once in a while I catch myself hum-
ming or singing a favorite hymn or just an alleluia when I am
alone.

Pray alone. Jesus was with people a great deal of the
time but He was also, I think, a very private person. He
needed to be alone. He needed time alone for prayer. Often in
the Gospels we read that He went off by Himself--into the
desert, into the hills, to the Garden of Olives. We need to do
something like that, too. Jesus tells us to go to our room, close
the door, and pray to our Father in private. And Jesus is
careful to assure us that our Father, who sees what others
cannot see, will repay us.

Pray in Liturgy. Liturgical prayer is not always easy
for us. In some ways, in fact, it is rather foreign. For instance,
in liturgical prayers, we often are not speaking directly to God
but rather to one another about God. This is strange to us. We
say or sing, "Glory to God in the highest." We do not say,
"Glory to you, O God, in the highest." In this kind of prayer
we are witnessing to one another. I remember hearing something on this kind of prayer once. It may sound irreverent but
it need not be. "We don't have to tell God how good God is;
God knows it!" But it is good for us to tell one another how
good God is and how much God has done for us. So we praise
God to one another.

Pray using visual aids. Many parishes now have
Liturgical Arts or Environment Committees. They plan and
prepare visual aids for liturgical prayer. We can do something
like that at home, too. We can use a Bible, a candle, a crucifix,
some other religious symbol, or something from nature. I
recently obtained a copy of that incredibly beautiful picture of
the planet Earth taken from an Apollo space mission. I have
framed and hung it and tell people it is my new "holy picture."

These visual aids can help us focus our attention. They can be aids to prayer.

Pray in action. An act of kindness is a prayer. In fact, we can say that without this kind of prayer in action our prayers in words are rather hollow. The Scriptures frequently remind us of this. Look at the prophet Isaiah, chapter one or chapter fifty-eight. Or take the first letter of John or the letter of James. And I am sure you are acquainted with the twenty-fifth chapter of the Gospel according to Matthew in which Jesus speaks of coming at the end time. He says He will separate the sheep from the goats, and the basis for the separation will be whether people have acted to help others. These are a few of the passages in the Scriptures which indicate how much God wants our prayer to be more than words alone. Prayer is a way of life. This, I think, is what Jesus means when He tells us to pray always.

Pray by centering. This may require a little explanation. Although this is an ancient form of Christian prayer, the name is new. A simple method of centering prayer is this. Choose a place and time to be quiet, perhaps seated in a comfortable chair. Close your eyes and relax. Try to relax your entire body, especially your face, neck, and shoulders. Breathe deeply and slowly. Then "center down," down into the center of your being. There God is! Jesus tells us that if we love Him, the Father will love us and they will come and make their dwelling with us. Focus attention on that Presence and "sum it up" with a word or simple phrase. Some people use "Jesus"; others, "Love" or "Friend." There should be no effort at thought, but there should be no anxiety when thoughts come. Simply put them aside and return to the Presence through the breathing and your word. When you wish to "come out" of your prayer, do it slowly just as you entered it slowly. You can do this by praying the Lord's Prayer deliberately and reflectively.

All praying has difficulties. When we pray with formulas, the challenge is to make sure we mean what we say. When we pray with our own prayers, the challenge is to do what Father Edward Farrell says in his book *Prayer Is a*

Hunger, and that is to pray from the bottom of our hearts, not from the top of our heads. But even if prayer is difficult, it is worth doing. The God we believe in is worth the time.

The story is sometimes told of a wise old monk, known for his wisdom in spiritual matters, who used to tell those who came to him, "Pray as you can, but pray!" That is probably a word of wisdom for all of us.

Peace!

Father Ed

QUESTIONS FOR REFLECTION OR DISCUSSION

1. One writer has said of prayer that we need to be willing to "waste time with God." What do you understand by this?
2. Is there a kind of prayer that is especially difficult for you-- for example, prayer of sorrow, of thanks, of quiet time with God?

11

THE CHRISTMAS I BELIEVE IN

Dear Friends,

For me, Christmas is not merely a feast day; it's a season, a mood, a pair of glasses, a way of seeing the world, and much more. I'm sure you've seen the picture of planet Earth taken on one of the Apollo missions. It is a picture of indescribable beauty, mostly brilliant blues and degrees of white, against the solid black background of space. That picture, I think, has forever changed the way people think of Earth. The Christmas I believe in is like that and more.

The Christmas I believe in has forever changed the world. Some of the things associated with Christmas are not the real Christmas or at least the Christmas I believe in. I don't believe in the Christmases of the full-page advertisements and the decorated stores, the commercial boon. I don't believe in the Christmases which are only tinsel and lights, gaudy displays and overstuffed Santas on the corners--Santas with their fake beards, their phony HoHoHos and their red-nosed reindeer. I don't believe in the Christmases of the office parties and their excesses or the gift-giving which is not really giving but a very calculated exchange. I don't believe in the Christmases of some of the sentimental carols and cards. In short, I don't believe in Christ-less Christmases.

The Christmas I do believe in begins with Advent. Not four weeks, but with Advent in the sense that we are aware that something is missing, something is incomplete, something is broken and needs fixing--in myself, in those around me, in our world.

Years ago, Steve Allen had a comedy routine on television entitled "The Question Man." He would be presented with a name or a statement, and then he would formulate a question which might have called for that name or statement as its answer. The Christmas I believe in is an answer. To appreciate it, we need to have a sense of the question. If Jesus is to be a Savior to us, we need to know that we are in trouble. We have an expression: *If it ain't broke, don't fix it*. If Jesus is to fix us, we need to recognize our brokenness and the brokenness in so much of our world.

The Christmas I believe in is not only about the past. It is that, but not only that. It is about now and about us, and it is also about the future. The Christmas I believe in is the birth of the Son of God who came to us as Savior. From that time on, every woman, every child, and every man can say: God has become, God is, one of us!

Because of Christmas, God is one of us and because God is one of us, we are special.

The Christmas I believe in changes everything. It changes every one of us, gives us a new dignity and worth. St. Augustine wrote, "God became man that men might become gods." That's very strong language! Even when we spell that word with a small "g," that's a powerful thought--that we might become gods!

Because the Christmas I believe in changes us, it also changes all of our relationships. Because of Christmas, every person--the sales clerk, the auto mechanic, the waitress, the teacher--has a divine dignity and deserves to be treated in accord with that dignity. Because of Christmas, God is one of us and, because God is one of us, we are special.

The Christmas I believe in is a call to forgiveness and peace--between friends, in families, among all peoples and nations. This is the reason that for many years the popes have issued peace proposals at Christmas. The Christmas I believe in is a call to peace.

The Christmas I believe in is not merely sentiment and softness, although sentiment can be good. In its call to forgiveness, it is also a challenge. In Jesus, in the first Christmas, the God we sinned against made the first move toward us, toward reconciliation. The sinned against came to the sinner. The Christmas I believe in says I must be willing to make the first move to those who have sinned against me. The Creator has come to the creature. The Christmas I believe in says the parent should be willing to come with forgiveness to the child, the principal to the student, the employer to the employee. The Christmas I believe in doesn't make sense; it goes beyond. It is the foolishness of love. The Christmas I believe in is a story of a prodigal God who offers love to all, worthy and unworthy. The Christmas I believe in is truly about the wonders of God's love.

The Christmas I believe in tells us something of the past, of course, of how God came into our world and our lives. It also gives us a message for the present. And the Christmas I believe in gives us a forecast for all future days. This Jesus who came as an infant in Bethlehem would later, as the Risen Christ, be able to say, "I am with you all days even to the end of the world." Jesus Christ, who is the same yesterday, today, and forever.

The Christmas I believe in is both sad and joyful. It is sad because "He came to what was His own, but His own people did not accept Him" (John 1:11). There was no room for Him in the inn when He was born so He was born in a stable outside the city. And, we remember, He died on a cross on Calvary, a hill outside the city. But the Christmas I believe in is also, and especially, joyful. People who believe have served the poor, worked and suffered for justice and peace, proclaimed the good news--all in the name of Jesus. And the last chapter of the Bible, in the Book of Revelation, says that those who have washed their robes--that is, those who have changed their lives--will enter the city, the New Jerusalem. In one of my favorite hymns, we sing, "Let us build the city of God." We can do this, we can build the city of God, because of the Christmas I believe in.

The Christmas I believe in says that Jesus is for everyone. In the Gospel according to St. Matthew, the Magi, apparently educated and wealthy, were led to Jesus by a star. The shepherds were quite different. They appear in the Gospel according to St. Luke. They were practically outcasts. They could not testify in court. They had the kind of reputation that might cause people to ask, "Would you want your sister to marry one?" The Christmas I believe in welcomes the outcasts, even sends angels to invite them.

The Christmas I believe in tells us that we are all poor before God. We all come with empty hands. We come, thirsting and hungry, in need of nourishment. And the Christmas I believe in announces that Jesus was laid in a manger, the place of food for cattle. This Jesus is food. Jesus says:

> "One does not live by bread alone,
>   but by every word that comes forth
>   from the mouth of God."
>   Matthew 4:4

In Christmas, Jesus is the Word-made-flesh. And Jesus is food in yet another way. He assures us, "...The bread that I will give is my flesh for the life of world" (John 6:51). Take and eat, He says, take and drink. My flesh is real food. My blood is real drink. The Christmas I believe in is both a beginning and unfinished business. So many have not been fed with the Word, so many are hungry in body, so many remain without rooms in our inns. So many inside the boundaries of our cities are outside the life of the city. All of us are without the fullness of the peace that Jesus, Prince of Peace, came to bring.

If we think of Christmas as a beginning, as unfinished business, we also have to think of the frightening numbers of abortions in our country and of the attitudes and values they express. In the birth of Jesus, we see the dignity of human life. That dignity, which belongs to every human life at every stage of life, is still not appreciated and respected in our world. The Christmas I believe in is a call to everyone of us to take time to reflect on the Infant who lay in the crib in Bethlehem and to come to a deeper appreciation of the preciousness of human life--because God has become one of us.

The Christmas I believe in gives us Mary, the Mother of Jesus, quiet, strong, and faithful. Mary is the only adult who appears in the Gospel stories of the birth of Jesus and also appears in the stories of the public life of Jesus. And she is there under the cross. She is there from beginning to end. What Mary is, we, the Church, are called to be.

So you can see that the Christmas I believe in is not only past but also present and even future. In Jesus, the Word was made flesh. That Christmas is past. The Word, God's Word, is to become flesh also in you and me. That Christmas is now and the future.

Christmas Peace!

Father Ed

QUESTIONS FOR REFLECTION AND DISCUSSION

1. How can we observe an ongoing Advent in the sense of deepening our awareness that we need a Savior?
2. If we believe that Christmas confers a new dignity on every human being, how will this affect our relationships with others?
3. The Infancy Narratives include people of different classes and social standing, animals, angels, and even nature in the guidance of the star. What significance do you see in this?

12

THE EASTER I BELIEVE IN

Dear Friends,

Throughout this season of Lent, the Church has been asking us to prepare for our celebration of Easter. The Easter I believe in is a message. It is a feast, too, of course--a celebration. But celebrations are messages written with all capital letters, with many exclamation points. Celebrations are messages with music and song and, often, with dancing. Celebrations call for dress-up clothes and decorations. Celebrations have food and drink. Above all, celebrations need people, and when the people gather, they tell stories. We have all of these in the Easter I believe in. In this letter, I want to share with you something of what I believe about Easter.

Sometime ago, I had a phone call from a woman wanting to arrange for the Baptism of her newborn baby. After congratulating her, I explained that we would not have any Baptisms in the season of Lent and that the next Baptism date in the parish would be Easter. At that she said, "Oh, that's a nice day!" She was partly right. I think, however, that it's important not only to be right but to be right for the right reason. I'm not sure she was. And I say "partly" right because Easter is not just a nice day for Baptism, it is *the* day. I'm not sure that all of us, like that young mother, appreciate the reason why.

First of all, I'd like to reflect on some of the Easters I

don't believe in. I don't believe in an Easter where the focus is on colored eggs and egg hunts or on cards with saccharine verses whose lines end with cheap rhymes. I don't believe in the Easters when the first topic is, "What did the Easter bunny bring you?" I don't believe in the Easters that become fashion shows which do not express new life so much as a bank account or a credit line. I don't believe in an Easter which is celebrated without faith.

I remember that one of the first bits of theologizing my grade school friends and I did went something like this: If God is all-powerful, can He make a stick with one end? If He can't, it seems that He is not all-powerful. The fact that a stick with only one end is a contradiction in terms was a little beyond us at that time. If we had thought in bigger terms, we might have asked: Can God make a bridge with one end? Even God cannot make a bridge with only one end.

The Easter I believe in is one end of a bridge. The other end of the bridge is Lent. And the three days of Holy Thursday to Easter Sunday, which we call the Triduum, are the center of the bridge. Triduum means three days, but they form a unity. They celebrate the Passover Mystery, Jesus' passing over from death to life. Lent is the time of preparing for our own passing over: not just our final and definitive death, but all the dyings and risings, all the experiences we have of letting go and leaving behind so that we can enter the new.

So, the Easter I believe in begins with Lent. But there are also Lents I do not believe in. I don't believe in a Lent which is to make up for our sins. Jesus has done that! I remember the Lents of my childhood when we thought of this season as a time to give up candy, desserts, or movies. Then, because adults didn't have to fast on Sundays, some of us children figured we could have our candy and other things on Sunday, too. But most of all we waited for Holy Saturday at noon when the Lenten fast was over. Then we could have the candy we had saved up throughout the forty days! I don't believe in that kind of Lent because it does not lead to the Easter I believe in. I don't believe in a Lent which is seen by itself, simply a time of deprivation, a Lent which is a dying, period. I don't believe in a Lent which is one end of a bridge that does not cross over to the other side. I don't believe in a Lent which does not have an Easter.

The Lent I believe in is the leading edge of a bridge, the first stage of a process. It is a dying which leads to new life. The Lent I believe in is not just an unpleasant idea, something that a vindictive God thought up, or that an authoritarian Church uses to exercise control. The Lent I believe in is necessary. The old must give way or the new cannot come into being. There is no spring without autumn or winter. Jesus says, "I solemnly assure you, unless the grain of wheat falls to the earth and dies, it remains just a grain of wheat. But if it dies, it brings forth much fruit" (John 12:24).

So, there must be a dying in order to come to new life. At a workshop this past year, someone said that people sometimes ask, "Is there life after death?" We should also ask, "Is there life before death?" Jesus tells us that the fullness of life comes only after a dying.

The new life that comes out of death can be for the person who has died, but it can also be for others. Jesus died--it's not quite accurate to say "and came back to life"--and passed over to new life. St. Paul tells us we are baptized into the dying of Jesus so that we may also rise to new life with Him.

In the early Church, most of the Baptisms were of adults. At first, these took place in rivers or streams. Jesus was baptized by John in the River Jordan. (This, of course, was not our sacrament of Baptism.) Then, rather early in its history, the Church introduced baptismal pools. These pools had two sets of steps. One set was used to enter the pool, the other to come out. The person being baptized did not simply go down into the pool and come back out to the same place, just as Jesus did not die and come back to the same kind of life. The person entered the pool from one side, was baptized, passed through the waters, and came up out of the pool on the other side. This symbolized the dying to one's former way of life and the beginning of a new way of life. The person then put on a new white robe, a symbol of the new person the baptized had become in Christ. This may also be the origin of the custom of new clothes at Easter.

The new life that comes out of death can be for the person who has died. It can also be for others. Jesus died, and out of His death, new life is possible for all of us. And that is why many parishes have programs during Lent like GDA (Give the Difference Away), the Love Loaves, or Operation Rice Bowl. All of these combine the idea of some form of sacrifice with the giving of the savings to help the poor. Out of our little dyings, new life for others can be made possible.

If our Lenten dying is giving up some of our free time to serve the needs of others, we may not have extra money to give away but our service itself will bring new life. Only out of death can new life come, for ourselves and for others. Unless the grain of wheat dies, it remains just a grain of wheat.

Our Lenten dying can also include accepting the sufferings, the weaknesses, the limitations--what one writer calls the "sore points"--in our lives. Then we will be able, perhaps even unconsciously, to reach out to others in their suffering. When we do that, both they and we are enriched.

The Lent and the Easter I believe in have to be seen together. They are two ends of the bridge we call the Passover Mystery.

Someone has said that we Christians are a people defined by our feasts and seasons. If that is true, and I think it is, then we are defined most of all by Lent and Easter. Lent and Easter celebrate the central mystery of our faith: the dying and rising of Jesus. Lent and Easter are the pivotal feast and season of our Church year.

...one of the earliest names for Christians was "the people of the Way."

We are defined, then, as a Passover people. The *Dogmatic Constitution on the Church* of Vatican II calls us a pilgrim people. And one of the earliest names for Christians was "the people of the Way." Both of these indicate that we are on a journey and we begin it, our passing over, our dying and rising, in the waters of Baptism. The whole of our time on earth, not just the forty days of Lent, is to be a continuation of that process of dying and rising begun in Baptism. So long as we live on earth, this process is never completed. And it is never too late to begin.

I recently heard an amazing story. The tomb of an ancient Egyptian king, dating five thousand years ago, was opened. In the tomb was a small container with a handful of seeds. Someone planted them, watered them, and placed them in sunlight. And they sprouted! If the power to come to new life is so great in nature, think of what it must be in the order of grace. Jesus tells us that His Word is a seed. It takes only some receptivity, some openness, to that word and it brings forth new life. I not only believe this; I have seen it. I have seen people profoundly transformed through the word, moving, for instance, from an uninvolved and basically self-centered life-style to one of service to others and work for justice. When this takes place, it is both amazing and beautiful.

Father John Shea says that Jesus is an offer that we can refuse. And he says that in this offer there is a kind of Catch-22. If we accept the offer, we will die. If we refuse the offer, we will die. But if we accept Jesus, that death will lead to new life.

The Gospels tell us of people who met the offer which Jesus is and refused. There was the rich young man with many possessions. He did not want to let go of these, and he went away sad. In the Gospel accounts, we read that some of the Pharisees received uncounted invitations to accept Jesus. They stubbornly refused. At the end of Jesus' life, Pilate had the offer which Jesus is and he, too, refused. These were all afraid, or, at least unwilling, to die to what they were or to let go of what they had. They did not come to new life. They did not cross the bridge.

But, you know, I believe the Gospels are, above all, good news. They tell us of many who met Jesus and accepted the offer that He is. Think of the woman at Jacob's Well. She had

had five husbands, although probably little love. She met and accepted Jesus. She left behind the empty water jar, symbol of her past life. With enthusiasm she went back into town and proclaimed to her neighbors that Jesus is the Messiah. Bishop Richard Sklba, a Scripture scholar, says that modern Scripture scholars think that the Samaritan Church was founded by her. Through her dying to her former way of life, she came to new life and she brought new life to others.

Think of Peter. He was so sure of himself. On the night Jesus was betrayed, Jesus predicted the betrayal and His own death. Peter, with the cocksure attitude so typical of him, said, "Even though I have do die with you, I will never disown you." Only a few hours later, Peter was challenged by a servant girl and denied that he even knew Jesus. Later on, when he had acknowledged his weakness and sin--we might say, accepted his sore point--he was healed and given new life. In that new life, he could acknowledge Jesus, not merely before a servant girl, but before the high priests, the elders, and all the leaders of the people. These men had the power to arrest him, put him in prison, and beat him.

There is one more thing I would like to mention regarding the Lent and Easter I believe in. It's called the RCIA, the Rite of Christian Initiation of Adults. At one time, the Mass was divided into the Mass of the Catechumens and the Mass of the Faithful. In the early centuries, those who wanted to become Christians were called catechumens. They were dismissed from the assembly at the end of that first part of the Mass, which we now call the Liturgy of the Word. The catechumenate frequently extended over a number of years, but it always culminated in a more intense process during Lent. In recent years, the Church has re-instated the catechumenate under this new name, the RCIA. It, too, can extend over a long period of time. It, too, becomes more intense during Lent.

The period of Lent as observed in the RCIA is not so much a period of growth in information about the Church as it is a time of formation, or conversion. It is for the catechumens, as it is for all of us, a time of dying to one way of life and coming to a new one. Even though you and I are already baptized and are trying to live the Christian way, Lent can and should be a special time for us in the ongoing conversion and growth which is the Christian life.

So, the Lent and Easter I believe in is not a trip into history. We are not simply recalling the dying and rising of Jesus two thousand years ago. His personal passover, it is true, is history. Ours, however, is in process. He is a model for us. We are His followers.

We, all of us, are a pilgrim people. We are crossing a bridge, dying and rising, letting go and coming to be. My prayer for you, for myself, and for all the world is that we may continue to die to what is less and come to life in what is more, in Christ Jesus.

Easter Peace!

Father Ed

QUESTIONS FOR DISCUSSION OR REFLECTION

1. Can you think of "dyings" you have experienced that led to newness of life--for you? For others? Discuss.
2. Father Shea speaks of Jesus as an offer that can be refused. In addition to the examples given, think of other people in the Gospels who refused or who accepted the offer Jesus is. Which ones can you relate to? Why?

13

THE CONVERSION I BELIEVE IN

Dear Friends,

I have heard people mention that they are sometimes confused when they hear others talk about conversion because the word seems to mean different things to different people.

As Catholics, we have had the custom of using the word *converts* to refer to adults who enter our Church. Sometimes these people have been well-informed and active members of another Christian Church. Often, too, they bring with them an admirable love and knowledge of the Bible. To speak of them as converts could be an affront to that Church and to their participation in it.

In another sense, to speak of the change as a conversion may be too optimistic. If this sounds contradictory, let me explain. In my early years as a priest, I spent most of my evenings giving "convert instructions"--usually to one person at a time. I even had people on a waiting list. Then we priests of the parish decided to start a "convert class." Here we gathered the people for group instructions, gave them a book to read and study, and even administered some tests. When we were finished, we received them into the Church. Statistics, not only from our parish but also nationally, indicated that the majority of the people received into the Catholic Church that way did not persevere as active Catholics. Can we truthfully say that such a change from one church affiliation to another is a conversion?

A few years ago a young man came to the rectory to register as a member of the parish. In the course of our visit, he told me he had been a drug addict but that he had accepted Jesus as his personal savior and was cured of his addiction. He also told me that he had not completed high school and did not have a job. Before leaving, he said he would like to do some work in the parish, and I assumed he was offering to help with the cleaning of the buildings or the upkeep of the grounds. "Oh, no!" he said. What he wanted to do was to teach. I thanked him for the offer and told him that I would have to get to know him a little better and also to see him in church on Sundays for a while. I never saw the young man again. Had he experienced a conversion? I hope he had, but I don't know.

The conversion I believe in means first of all coming to a new way of thinking.

The conversion I believe in is a religious experience; it is, therefore, a response to God's call, which is grace. The conversion I believe in is usually not a dramatic event. Most often it is not even an event as we usually understand that word. It is a hardly discernible process, a change that is gradual. Even so, there can be special moments of grace in our lives that involve a significant step forward. But the process goes on. The conversion I believe in is a living out of what is begun when it is ritualized, celebrated, in Baptism: a process of dying and rising in Christ.

The Greek word, *metanoia*, is often used to describe conversion. The word is frequently translated as "a change of heart." It is more accurately translated as "a change of mind." The Prodigal Son, we are told, "came to his senses." We need to know before we can choose. The conversion I believe in means first of all coming to a new way of thinking. Accepting Jesus as one's personal Savior means accepting Jesus' teaching, His way of thinking. This takes time. It also takes study.

Christian theology has an ancient principle: grace builds upon nature; it does not supplant it. This means that if we have a broken arm, we should not only pray for healing, we should also seek medical assistance. It means that if we are self-centered and selfish, we need to strive to develop the virtues of love and service, as well as to pray for them.

In recent times, I have seen a number of articles on conversion which describe various areas of our lives that need to be changed if we are to have a true, holistic conversion. Some of these articles give a long list of areas but I want to mention a few of the areas I think are important.

The conversion I believe in is an affective one. This means a movement from a blockage or denial of our feelings to an acceptance of them. Some of us, especially men in our country, have been conditioned to try to repress all feelings. "Boys don't cry," we are told and, of course, the macho man is above such displays of feeling. The conversion I believe in is a move toward accepting feelings as a part of being human, seeing them as "standard equipment" for men as well as for women and children.

In counseling sessions, I have often had people say, "I know I shouldn't feel this way." No one needs to say that. Feelings are neither good nor bad; they just are. It is what we do with feelings that is either good or bad. The first thing that we must do with feelings is accept them as normal. After that, we can learn to express them in suitable and constructive ways.

I recall a talk in a marriage enrichment course. The speaker told this story about himself. He was a marriage counselor and became angry, not at the couples who came to him, but at the fact that at the time of their wedding, many of them were not prepared for marriage. He turned that anger into constructive action: he formed a group that presents marriage preparation and marriage enrichment programs. In the conversion I believe in, we also become more sensitive to the feelings of other people, and we learn to respond to their needs. We come to know that there are times to laugh and there are times to cry, times to be serious and times to lighten up, times to work and times to relax, times to be firm and times to bend.

When I was in the seminary, one of our professors wrote a booklet on the appeal to the emotions in preaching. That booklet was an exception. In general, we priests are head-trip people. Ideas and logic are our thing. I believe ideas and logic are very important, but today we are rediscovering the effectiveness of storytelling in our teaching and preaching. We know from the Gospels that Jesus was a master storyteller. Stories touch emotions: they motivate. If we are to be converted in the full sense of the word, we need to be converted to the acceptance of our emotions and to appropriate ways of expressing them.

The conversion I believe in is also intellectual. In intellectual conversion we come to realize the complexity of truth. Most of us, I fear, tend to be simplistic. We find it hard to keep the elements of truth in balance. Most, if not all, of our heresies have erred by overemphasis on one side of a complex issue.

The intellectual conversion I believe in recognizes also that truth can be expressed in different ways: in poetry, in symbol, in art, and in story. Intellectual conversion allows us to appreciate the beauty and richness of literature, especially the literature we call the sacred Scriptures. In Genesis, for example, we read that God walked with Adam and Eve in the cool of the day. We can read that literally and it is beautiful. We can also reflect that the cool of the day, the time after the day's work is done, is the time when friends can come together. Now, we see, cool of the day says much more; it speaks of an intimacy between God and creatures. Intellectual conversion allows us to understand more deeply the gift God gives us in sacraments. These are not theological statements but signs and symbols.

The conversion I believe in is also a change which is called religious conversion. Religious conversion is not primarily the accepting of a list of shoulds and shouldn'ts. It leads one rather to understand that religion came to be when human beings began to ask the big question: what is life all about? It leads one to acknowledge God not only as a power or even as a creator, but as a loving person who gives meaning to life. Religious conversion leads to prayer.

This conversion is far-reaching. It gives one a reason to get up in the morning, a reason to turn off the tube, a reason to pick up the Bible and read and, like Mary, to treasure these things and to ponder them in one's heart.

This religious conversion is described touchingly by a woman who completed the RCIA process and was baptized on a Cherokee reservation. She writes:

Will you take us now and make us useful?
Can we share these treasures?
Water and wine for a thirsty time--
Bread and roses for hungry hearts.
As you gave life for life
As life has been shared with us for life
So now we give our days and strength
To walk each gifted year around
In joy.

The conversion I believe in is also moral. Some students of human behavior have marked out various stages of moral development. One of the earliest sees the evil of an action as measured solely by the effect. In this way, the child who breaks four cups accidentally thinks this is more evil than to break one by throwing it down in anger. Another stage of moral development sees law as the norm. What the law forbids is wrong.

The moral conversion I believe in goes beyond law. It moves one to do good simply because it is good. Moral conversion attempts to take in the whole of life--not merely what is sexual. It begins to see the uneven distribution of this world's goods, poverty in the midst of riches, and racism, sexism, and all forms of discrimination as evil. The moral conversion I believe in sees us as stewards who are responsible for all of creation and its welfare. Moral conversion means growing in concern for the environment--for clean air, pure water, and rich soil--because these are given by our loving God to all persons equally, including those who will come after us.

The conversion I believe in is a Christian conversion. Christian conversion means moving from seeing Jesus only as an historical figure into nurturing a personal relationship with Him. Jesus often asked questions, and I think that one of the most important was, "Who do you say that I am?" In Christian conversion we try to face that question in the depths of our consciousness. By the way we live, who do we say, really, that Jesus is?

There is a little story about a believer and an unbeliever who were having a discussion. The believer insisted that Jesus is the Son of God and Messiah. The unbeliever walked to a window and stood there looking out over a busy street for a long time. Finally, he turned to the believer and said, "I don't see any difference."

The Christian conversion I believe in will make a difference. Jesus says, "By this shall all know that you are my disciples, if you have love for one another." In Baptism we put on Christ, His way of thinking and acting. Christian conversion makes a difference.

The conversion I believe in is ecclesial; it has to do with the Church. I often meet people who say, "I believe in God," or, "I am a Christian," or, "I am a Catholic" and then, "I just don't go to church." In ecclesial conversion we come to see the union of Jesus and the community of His followers, the Church. Jesus said to Paul, who was persecuting the Christian community, "Why are you persecuting me?" The ecclesial conversion I believe in means more than joining or simply belonging to a Church. In ecclesial conversion we do not ask, "Why doesn't the Church...?" We see ourselves as Church and ask, "Why don't we...?"

The early Christians spoke of Jesus as sacrament--sign of the presence of God in our world. Later, they realized that the Church is the sacrament of Jesus, of His continuing presence in the world. But this does not mean only the Church "out there." The ecclesial conversion I believe in helps us see the parish as the local sacrament of Jesus and, finally, it helps us see ourselves, you and me, as sacraments, signs of

Christ.

So, my friends, the conversion I believe in is not only for those who are not Catholics or for big sinners. It is a call to all of us. This kind of many-sided conversion is a process, it takes time, it makes a difference, and, so long as we live, it is never finished.

Peace!

Father Ed

QUESTIONS FOR REFLECTION AND DISCUSSION

1. As you look back over some years, can you see conversion in your life:

- *In relation to accepting feelings?*
- *In seeing that simple answers are not adequate for complex problems?*
- *In seeing that religion is not primarily shoulds and shouldn'ts?*

2. If conversion is first of all a change of mind, what helps to conversion most appeal to you:

- *Reading the Bible?*
- *Participation in a small group?*
- *Listening to talks?*

Discuss.

14

THE SPIRITUALITY I BELIEVE IN

Dear Friends,

Something interesting and, I think, significant is happening in our world. The sociologists and those who study trends in society tell us that there is an increasing interest in spirituality. Retreat centers, too, report greater numbers attending their programs. Because I was asked recently to give a talk on spirituality and had to clarify my own thinking on the matter, I thought you might like to see something of my approach.

First of all, there is no commonly accepted definition of spirituality. A seminary professor who teaches a course on the subject told me that he has collected about two hundred definitions. We can say that everyone has a spirituality in the broadest sense of the word. In this understanding, spirituality can be described as the way we organize our life, or as the principles that guide us in our actions. In this sense, a very greedy person has a spirituality. A lazy person has a spirituality. We might say that a greedy person guides his or her life by the principle: *What* can I get out of it, and the lazy person, by the principle: *How* can I get out of it. Obviously, I don't believe in spiritualities of greed and laziness. I do not claim that I am never greedy or lazy, but I think I can honestly say that I do not make those the principles around which I organize my life and actions.

There are other spiritualities, closer to what we usually think of as spirituality, that I do not believe in. There is a spirituality that assumes that we have to win God over by doing difficult things, painful things. I don't believe in such a spirituality. This is not to say that difficult things can never be good or helpful. Fasting and other forms of penance can be good, not because they are needed to change God, but because they can help change us. I can't believe in a spirituality that thinks God is pleased by human suffering because that implies things about God that I cannot believe.

Another spirituality I cannot accept is one that sees pleasure as evil. I recall an occasion in the seminary when a professor said something that I don't think I will ever forget or ever believe. He was talking about the old-time fruit cellars which were common on farms years ago. They were pungent with the aromas of many kinds of stored foods. He said, "I sometimes think that the pleasure one receives from entering a farmer's fruit cellar is almost sinful." I'm sure that he didn't mean that literally, but I can't believe in a spirituality that says such a pleasure is sinful.

I don't believe in a spirituality that seems to deny human responsibility, that says that all that we have to do is pray, have faith, and leave everything up to God. Nor do I believe in a spirituality which is the opposite, which holds that we can do it all on our own. This may be a special temptation for us North Americans. We are justly proud of our achievements. We have a "can do" attitude. Expressions such as "No problem" and "I can handle that" occur frequently in our conversations. We need to recognize that there are things that we cannot do on our own. I do not, for example, believe in a spirituality which says we can eliminate all our faults and grow in virtue entirely by our own efforts.

I don't believe in a spirituality which seeks its nourishment principally in extraordinary signs. This is the spirituality of private revelations and miraculous cures. I believe that God can do all things and that God continues to work wonders, but I do not think that we should organize our lives around the expectation of the extraordinary. I do not believe in traveling great distances to see weeping statues of Mary or images which people say are pictures of Jesus mysteriously appearing on walls. I do believe, however, that God works in marvelous ways in our lives. God does this in the Church, in God's word, in sacraments, through other people, and even in ordinary events. We need to grow in the ability to see God wherever God comes into our lives. We need to see God in the splendors of nature, the wondrous event of the birth of a child, the awesome complexity and beauty of our bodies and their organs, the almost infinite potential of our minds, the capacity of our souls to accept and return love, the quiet time we have with family and friends.

Let me mention one more spirituality I don't believe in, a spirituality of numbers. We used to emphasize nine First Fridays, five First Saturdays, nine of all sorts of prayers to form a novena. Because our God is a God of love, I can't believe that the numbers are that important. Jesus told Peter not to limit his forgiving to seven times but rather to forgive seventy times seven times. In this, Jesus is saying, "Don't keep count." Numbers are not important, but forgiving and praying are.

There are other spiritualities that I don't believe in, but I want to tell you about the spirituality I do believe in. More and more, as I reflect on my own life, I think that my spirituality is one of stewardship. I am keenly aware of the fact that everything I have is something I have received, and received ultimately from God. Everything is gift, and God wants me to use my gifts according to God's overall plans. Stewardship embraces the use of my time, my care for my body, my ongoing study to improve my mind. It includes my love for the gifts I know as my family and friends. It looks to what I do with my money and how I treat the environment. It applies to the whole of my life and all of my relationships, attitudes, and actions. Most of all it applies to the gift of my faith and all that I have received from God through Christ. The stewardship that I, as a Christian, am called to exercise is stewardship of the gifts of Baptism.

The spirituality I believe in is, more than anything else, a baptismal spirituality. It is in Baptism that we are initiated into the Christian community. In the letter to the Romans, we read that Baptism plunges us into the death and resurrection of Jesus. In early Christian times, the Baptism ritual signed or symbolized, very dramatically, that process of dying and rising. Even though our Baptism may have involved only the pouring of a little water and not the dramatic ritual of the early Church, it is for us, too, a dying and rising. In Baptism we die to sin and are born into new life in Christ.

When I say that the spirituality I believe in is a baptismal spirituality, I mean that I think of this dying and rising as a process. In Christ, the dying and rising is complete. He has passed over, once for all, through death to new life. For us, it is only begun in Baptism. It is lived out in the whole of our lives.

With reflection, we can see that process going on continually in our own lives. For example, some of my transfers and other experiences as a priest were very painful. Later I came to realize that through those very experiences I have grown. Dying and rising. I have seen it also in others. I have, for example, ministered to many sick people. I have seen their illness, weakness, dependence on others become a dying that leads to new life--to patience, to prayer, and to a beautiful tranquillity. But this growth and new life is not automatic. We must accept it; we must embrace the cross. Otherwise, sickness can lead to bitterness, even despair. Nevertheless, I believe it is only because of the dying and rising of Christ that our dyings can be life-giving.

One of the pervasive illnesses in our society is alcoholism. Among alcoholics and those who work with them, the understanding is that an alcoholic has to "hit bottom" before he or she can begin to come back to a healthy way of life. The first step in Alcoholics Anonymous is for the alcoholic to recognize and accept that his or her life has become unmanageable. Only then can he or she progress on the road to sobriety and wholesome living. Dying and rising. There is a growing body of spiritual literature which sees the Twelve Steps of Alcoholics Anonymous as a valid basis not only for recovery from various addictions, but as a spirituality for all of us.

The spirituality I believe in recognizes the dying which is

going on in our lives and sees it as the work of God which calls for a response. That response is acceptance or surrender.

The spirituality I believe in goes further. In a sense, it leads us not only to accept the dyings that come into our lives but also to choose to die in some ways so that we may live in a new way. In the Baptism ceremony, we renounce Satan and all of his works. We choose to die to sin. We also profess our faith in God and God's Church. That's a rising.

Choosing to die sometimes means turning away even from what is good in order to choose what is better. Dying and rising. "Unless the grain of wheat falls to the earth and dies," Jesus says, "it remains just a grain of wheat. But if it dies, it produces much fruit." (See John 12:24.) Again, Jesus tells us, "Whoever would save his life will lose it, but whoever loses his life for my sake will find it." (See Matthew 16:25.) Dying and rising.

The spirituality I believe in is a spirituality of love. If we love others, we put them, their needs and best interests, ahead of us and ours. It is very difficult to love all persons. I remember hearing a talk once about the importance of breaking out of the habit of stereotyping. The speaker said that we need to see the *person* in others. We must see black *persons*, female *persons*, handicapped *persons*, welfare *persons*. Hearing that talk was a profoundly moving experience. The spirituality I believe in calls for us to die to our prejudices and pride and grow in loving others.

Sometimes, it seems, the people closest to us are the ones we find it most difficult to love--spouses, children, co-workers. We know their faults so well, and we see these faults more clearly than our own. It is here, especially, that dying to our self-centeredness is life-giving to others. The spirituality I believe in looks beyond oneself to the service of others. It is a spirituality of involvement: in the Church, in the neighborhood, and in the larger society in which we live. The spirituality I believe in sees that hunger and thirst for justice and peace is a part of the Gospel picture of the Christian life. Service is a kind of dying, and it is life-giving to others.

We don't usually do a thing well the first time we do it. The spirituality I believe in is a lifelong rehearsal in dying.

And what we usually call death, the experience of those whose names appear in the obituary columns, is not the first dying but the final and definitive dying. That dying leads to the final and definitive rising, a rising to full life and union with Christ.

Spirituality needs to be nourished. In Baptism, we receive the Holy Spirit, and the very word *spirituality* comes from the name of the Third Person of the Holy Trinity. All growth in the spirituality I believe in is the work, first of all, of the Holy Spirit. I believe that the Scriptures are inspired, "inspirited," and I find much nourishment for my spirituality in them: in reading them, in studying them, and reflecting on them, and in hearing them proclaimed in the Liturgy. Jesus, when He was tempted in the desert, said that we do not live on bread alone but on every word that comes from the mouth of God. (See Matthew 4:4.)

I find that the Eucharist and every sacramental celebration is a renewal of Baptism and a source of nourishment. I know I also need daily personal, private prayer to nourish my spiritual life. Finally, I find that I am fed and significantly strengthened spiritually in my relationships with those I love and who love me.

In the creation story in the book of Genesis, we read that God looked at all that God had made and saw that it was very good. Yet we believe that God calls us to an unimaginably more wonderful life in heaven. To go from this world to that is a dying and rising and the culmination of the spirituality I believe in.

Peace!

Father Ed

QUESTIONS FOR REFLECTION AND DISCUSSION

1. Reflect on your own spirituality--the guiding principle in your life. How would you describe it?
2. What are the sources of nourishment in your spiritual life?
3. How is working for justice and peace a part of a Christian's spiritual life?

15

THE HEAVEN I BELIEVE IN

Dear Friends,

It seems that we do not talk much about heaven, although at the time of someone's death, there may be some comments. Yet heaven is an experience we all hope to have for eternity. I think it is important for all of us to think about heaven, and so it might be good to tell you something about the heaven I believe in.

Unfortunately, the popular pictures of angels or former inhabitants of earth, floating around on clouds and playing harps, are not very attractive. If a one-hour Mass seems long to us, a never-ending heavenly liturgy is certainly not going to be very appealing. Neither is the idea of a place where the streets are paved with gold. After all, if we are in heaven, who needs gold? Nor do I find helpful the tired old jokes about St. Peter at the gate and the special enclosures for Catholics and Protestants. I don't believe in those kinds of heavens.

The heaven I believe in is the heaven we read about in the Scriptures, which tell us that eye has not seen, ear has not heard, nor has it so much as dawned on us what God has prepared for those who love God. (See 1 Corinthians 2:9.) That probably means that everything I say is going to be wrong! I do not think, however, that it means that thinking and dreaming about heaven has no value. What it certainly does mean is this wonderful truth: Our imaginations are too small, and even the best of our dreams about heaven are woefully short of the reality of what our God has planned.

One way I like to think about heaven is through the use of images. The heaven I believe in, for example, is a meal. When I say this, I do not intend to suggest that we should let our imaginations run wild about our favorite food and drink, and then multiply the amounts of that food and drink and our capacity to consume them to infinity. I think of the story of the little boy who didn't want to eat his vegetables. He was eyeing the pie they were to have for dessert. He told his mother that all the boxes in his stomach were filled except the dessert box. When I say the heaven I believe in is a meal, I do not mean that all of the "boxes" in our stomach will have an infinite capacity.

Actually, I think that in heaven, in our risen bodies, we will not need food. But a meal is much more than merely consuming food. Ideally, a meal is a family event or a gathering of friends who have become "family" for us. How often we say to a relative or friend we haven't seen for a while, "Let's get together for dinner sometime." The nourishment we receive from such meals is not limited to bodily nourishment. Our relationships, too, are nourished in our being together.

Think of all the good things that go on at meals with friends, at family gatherings, at banquets of celebration. Think of the pleasures and joys of remembering times shared, of good conversation and laughter. The heaven I believe in includes all of that. I am thinking of family get-togethers at which everyone who is invited manages to come, no one is sick, the conversation does not become boring or contentious, everyone's contributions are recognized and respected, and everyone is happy. Think of such a meal and then think of it as never having to end. That never happens, of course, here on earth. But that is one of the ways I think of the heaven I believe in.

Another image that helps describe the heaven I believe in is home. How often we say or hear someone say about those who have died, "They have gone home." Home! It is a special place, and the word *home* itself becomes special, also, and evokes rich memories and deep feelings. Home is much more than a house, although it usually includes one. Home is more than a neighborhood, although it usually includes that, too. It takes time for a house to become a home; it takes experiences --experiences of joy and pain--the blood, sweat, and tears of human living. Most of all, a home includes family and the special relationships we have in our family. A house does not have to have a history; a home does.

In recent years, we have seen the growth of the hospice program, a way of caring for the dying, and even more recently, the possibility of a home hospice. What a beautiful return to a former way for the terminally ill: People can die at home! Sometime ago, I was visiting with the family of a man who had the grace of dying in that way, at home. They said that he had a favorite expression when people who had come to see him were about to leave. "Come good home!" he would say to them. When we die, I think that is what our God says to us: "Come good home."

Heaven is God's home become ours. We should not think of it so much as our reward--we cannot earn heaven, it is always gift--but rather as the culmination of the life we have lived on earth. When we move into the heaven I believe in, we will not need time to get adjusted. We will feel right at home right away.

The heaven I believe in has the history of our life, our relationship with God and others, and it is all ready and waiting for us when we arrive. We know that God is with us here on earth, but I think we can all resonate with the thought of the child who said, "I know God is with me here, but I need a God with skin on." In the heaven I believe in, God will not have skin on, but our experience of being home with God will make skin unnecessary. If, in the heaven I believe in, we do not have hugs, we will have something even better. It is a great big happy homecoming of all of God's people.

The heaven I believe in is not like anything we know or even can imagine, and yet, it is in some way a continuation of life here on earth. Everything that God has made is good. In fact, everything God has made is *very* good. And nothing that is good and that we value will be lost in the heaven I believe in. All that is good and beautiful on earth will be there: the holy joys of loving relationships between spouses, relatives, and friends; the splendor of the natural world; the satisfaction of a life well-lived. And all this will be wrapped, magnified, intensified in our experience of the friendship we enjoy with God. Only the limitations of earthly relationships will be lost.

We read in the Book of Revelation:

"They will not hunger or thirst anymore,
    nor will the sun or any heat strike them.
For the Lamb who is in the center of the throne
        will shepherd them
and lead them to the springs of life-giving water,
    and God will wipe away every tear from their eyes."
Revelation 7:16,17

Above all, the relationship we have with God here on earth will be brought to perfection in the heaven I believe in, as we see in the First Letter of John: "Beloved, we are God's children now; what we shall be has not yet been revealed. We do know that when it is revealed we shall be like [God], for we shall see [God] as [God] is" (1 John 3:2).

I once heard a homily in which the priest told about traveling by train to visit a friend. He had just settled into his seat with a book when he was startled to hear a high-pitched "Wow!" He looked around and saw a boy of about four, with his face pressed tightly against the window. The boy was looking at the farmland, and when he saw a cow, he exclaimed, "Wow!" Then there were horses and sheep, and every time something new came into view, his delighted response was a loud "Wow!" One thing I am sure about is this: In the heaven I believe in there will be endless surprises. God has told us: It will always exceed anything we have seen or heard and even everything that has dawned on us.

People who are in love are happy people. The heaven I believe in is filled with people who are with the ones they love. In heaven, our love will transcend all the limitations, all the imperfections it suffers here on earth. Imagine a situation in which there is no difficulty in communicating, no misunderstanding, no envy or selfishness remaining in our hearts.

And this situation never ends. In the heaven I believe in, we will have perfect happiness.

The heaven I believe in is also the heaven of the frequent expressions of rest and peace. My guess is that the description of heaven as rest originated in an age when most people had to work hard physically. Heaven, then, would bring rest from those hard labors. But also in our day, I sense many people feel burdened in different ways, and a heaven of rest is very appealing. The God I believe in will give rest, eternal rest, in the heaven I believe in.

Then, too, I often hear people say of someone who has died, "She is at peace; he is at peace." In this situation, that word *peace* says so much. Sometimes I think it refers to the struggles of the person's last illness. When death is finally accepted, or overcomes that last human resistance, there is peace. Often, too, the word *peace* is a recognition that much of life on earth is a struggle and often involves painful conflict. Heaven, God's final and definitive gift, is a state of peace.

Some years ago, the novel *Love Story* became a best seller and later was made into a motion picture. Probably the most famous line in that show--famous because it was so stupid!--was, "Love means not ever having to say you're sorry." About that same time, I was asked by the Archdiocese to leave the parish I was serving--and which I loved very much--to assume the pastorate of another. It was a painful time for me and the people I was close to. I was open with the people about the pain of leaving them and saying goodbye. It was at this time that the thought occurred to me to adapt that infamous line from *Love Story*. The heaven I believe in, I told them, means not ever having to say good-bye.

Peace!

Father Ed

QUESTIONS FOR REFLECTION OR DISCUSSION

1. What images of heaven are most appealing to you? Why?
2. How can you talk to a little child about what heaven is like? An old person? A dying person?

16

THE SOCIAL TEACHING
I BELIEVE IN

Dear Friends,

I recently saw a book whose subtitle is *Our Best Kept Secret*. What is that secret? The book's main title tells us: *Catholic Social Teaching*. It reminds me of a poster I once saw in the window of a business establishment: "This is a non-profit organization. It wasn't meant to be, but that's what it is." In much the same way, Catholic social teaching was not meant to be a secret, but that's what it is. In my experience, a very small percentage of our people realize that the Church has a comprehensive body of social teaching. It seems that we who are teachers in the Church have either neglected to teach this doctrine or we have failed to communicate it effectively.

I think there is another possibility. It is related to one of the few things I remember from my study of the Greek language. The Greek word for "to hear" can have either of two meanings. Used one way, it means "to hear"; used another way, it means "to accept" or "to obey." I am afraid some people are not ready to hear, in the sense of to accept, the social teaching of the Church. For example, I recently participated in a small discussion group, and one of the questions was whether we agree with the assessment of Pope John Paul II that the environmental crisis is a religious issue. One man immediately spoke up and said that there is no crisis. He went on to say that there is no scientific proof that the ozone layer is being diminished; it is merely shifting around.

Some of the things he said may be true, but there are other factors in the environmental crisis. He had isolated one issue and, without offering any proof, simply denied it. I later learned a fact that may well have influenced his thinking. He is an employee of a company that has been in trouble for causing pollution. For him to accept the statement of the Pope would not be a matter of mere intellectual assent for him. It might have serious consequences in his way of life.

There are social teachings that I, too, do not believe in. I do not believe in social teachings that profess to have all the answers, simple ones at that, to all the complicated social problems of our day. I do not believe in a social teaching that divides people into classes and pits different groups against one another. And I do not believe in a social doctrine which is an entirely new body of teaching in the Church. Above all, I do not believe in a social teaching which may be interesting but is not really important to a Christian life.

The social teaching I do believe in is part of our Jewish-Christian tradition from the very first days of biblical times. It begins with the story of the creation of Adam and Eve. Again, I think of a poster. This one is a picture of a little boy in ragged clothes, against a slum background. The text of the poster reads, "God made me and God don't make junk." No person created by God is junk, and when we read on in the story of creation we find that there is more, much more, about the dignity, the value of the human person.

We read that God created human beings in God's own image. When we think about it, that is an absolutely astonishing statement. Every woman and every man has a divine dignity. This dignity of every human person is the basis for all the Catholic social teaching I believe in. In the morning, as I arise, I spend a few moments in prayer--before my regular morning prayer--and part of that first prayer is recalling this truth, thanking God for this gift of divine dignity, and asking God that I may never forget that I and everyone I will deal with this day have that divine dignity. And I hope I never get used to it!

There is much in the Hebrew Scriptures, our Old Testament, about the reverence we need to have for the dignity of men and women. The prophets called God's people to respect that dignity. If a poor man's cloak is taken as security for a loan, it is not to be kept overnight because he will need it to keep him warm as he sleeps. A day laborer's wages are not to be held back overnight, and to defraud a worker of his wages is one of the sins that cry to heaven for vengeance. The prophet Micah has a simple and beautiful summary of what is required of God's people:

> Only to do the right and to love goodness,
> and to walk humbly with your God.
>
> Micah 6:8

When we turn to the New Testament, we see that Jesus teaches both by word and by action. In the Gospel according to St. Luke, at the very beginning of Jesus' public life, in the synagogue of His hometown, Nazareth, He makes His own the words of the prophet Isaiah. He has come, He says, to proclaim liberty to captives, and recovery of sight to the blind, and to let the oppressed go free. And in His first instruction in Matthew, the Sermon on the Mount, Jesus says that the merciful and the peacemakers will be blessed. He goes on to say that we are to love all, even our enemies.

Later, when the hard-line legalists of His day criticize Him for curing on the Sabbath, He makes it clear that even the Sabbath, that most sacred day, is for us and not the other way around. No matter how hard an employer wants to work his laborers, the Sabbath is a sacred day of rest for them. Even so, Jesus will "work" on the Sabbath to remove a person's suffering. And when Jesus describes the Last Judgment, He does it in terms of social actions: feeding the hungry, clothing the naked, and welcoming the stranger.

Perhaps this is one of the reasons that Pope John Paul II says in his encyclical *Centesimus Annus* that social teaching is an essential part of the Christian message. Although Catholic social teaching has its origins in ancient writings, it also includes something new in modern times. Toward the end of the nineteenth century, Pope Leo XIII issued an encyclical in which he applied traditional social teachings to the new situations which had arisen from the industrial revolution. Since that time, succeeding popes and the United States bishops have frequently updated his first application of Catholic teaching to economic life.

Anything I say will be inadequate, but I would like to mention at least a few things about this crucial area. Because of their dignity, workers have a right to organize and to receive a wage that will support them and their families. They are to have safe working conditions, humane working hours, and rest. Men and women have equal rights. In recent years, the bishops of the United States wrote a pastoral letter entitled *Economic Justice for All*. In Chapter I, "The Church and the Future of the U. S. Economy," they applied these principles to economic life in the United States. They began by saying that we need to ask three questions: "What does the economy do *for* people? What does it do *to* people? And how do people *participate* in it?" For me, one of the document's most moving statements is this: "No one may claim the name Christian and be comfortable in the face of the hunger, homelessness, insecurity and injustice found in this country and the world." (#27)

Perhaps no area of our society is as emotional, divisive, even explosive, as that of racial relations. I have found it almost impossible to discuss this with a group without the fears and angers of the participants coming to the surface. We may hear stories of bizarre behavior, of welfare fraud, of decreased property values. It is important to remember that the people who tell these stories are not bad people. Sometimes they speak from experience, sometimes from false rumors, sometimes from ignorance. We need to deal with them with sensitivity and patience.

When I encounter such a situation, I often recall a talk by a very cultured black gentleman. In the question-and-answer session following his presentation, a woman rose and cited some statistics that contradicted his. In reply, he said, "Obviously, your figures and mine do not agree. I checked mine again just before coming here this evening. May I ask, Ma'am, did you check yours?" But most of all, we must also be faithful to our convictions. Catholic social teaching holds that the heart of the race question is religious and moral.

During the years of the Cold War, people all over the world lived in constant anxiety and apprehension over the possibility of another worldwide conflict, including the horror of using nuclear weapons. The Church continued to talk about the basis of true peace, which is justice. What helps me most of all in this area is this: The presumption is always for peace and against war. Perhaps the practice in American courts can help us understand this. In our courts, the defendant is presumed to be innocent unless he or she is proved, beyond a reasonable doubt, to be guilty. In a similar way, in the question of peace and war, the presumption is for peace. This means that in any given instance, we do not need to justify a stand for peace. Rather the burden of justification falls on those who favor military action.

I want to add just one more basic idea concerning the Catholic social teaching I believe in. It is called the preferential option for the poor. Following God's frequent expressions of concern for the poor, the weak, "the widow and the orphan" in Scripture, the Church says that in all things we need to show a preference for responding to the world's poor.

The social teaching of the Church is beautiful and compassionate. It is also challenging. When Jesus proclaims that He comes to bring good news to the poor, that can be, or at least can be seen to be, bad news for the rich. When He says that He comes to let the oppressed go free, that can be seen as bad news for the oppressors. That is why the prophets, those who challenge the leaders of their time, are persecuted and frequently killed. Priests, too, who faithfully preach Catholic social teaching can expect to meet opposition. When the powerless are empowered--by knowledge, by a sense of their own dignity, by a sense of solidarity with one another-- those in power are threatened.

The Catholic social teaching I believe in makes sense. It salvages human lives; it fosters a sense of dignity, worth, and accomplishment. It works for the common good. It also makes

99

sense in economic terms. We are told that regular maintenance of our cars, the furnaces in our homes, and the equipment in our offices saves money over the years. Likewise, one dollar spent in providing good nutrition for infants saves many dollars later in health care. One dollar spent in early education saves many dollars later in remedial education and even in court costs and imprisonment. I recently saw a day care sign: *It is easier to build a boy than to remake a man.* Investing in the care of children makes sense in every way.

I wanted to write to you about this even though I realized I could do no more than give you an introduction. An indication of the broad range of Catholic social teaching is found in *Political Responsibility*, a recent publication of the United States bishops. It applies Catholic social principles to seventeen public issues, listed alphabetically from abortion to substance abuse.

The Catholic social teaching I believe in is a challenge to all of us. It is a challenge to us who are teachers to see to it that it is no longer the Church's best-kept secret. It is a challenge to all of us to hear it in the sense of accepting and obeying it. It is no less than a challenge to follow Jesus, who had a special love for the suffering, the poor, the powerless.

Peace!

Father Ed

QUESTIONS FOR REFLECTION AND DISCUSSION

1. Which area of the Church's social teaching do you find most difficult to "hear," that is, to accept:

- *Equality of the sexes*
- *Economic justice*
- *Race relations*
- *Peace*

Why?

2. How can you help to spread knowledge of the Church's social teaching?

17

THE PEACE I BELIEVE IN

Dear Friends,

When the Berlin Wall came down and, later, when the Soviet Union was dissolved, many of us thought that peace had arrived. Or, at least, that it was just around the corner. Even now, however, humankind is plagued with wars and rumors of wars in many lands. Peace, true peace between nations all over the world, is still a hope, not a reality.

What is sad, too, is that many people do not have peace in themselves, in their families, and in their relationships with friends, neighbors, and co-workers. Perhaps saddest of all, we do not even have peace in our churches. It sometimes seems that the old devil of *Screwtape Letters* was right when he wrote that "to be is to be in competition." What has happened in our society, and what can we do about it?

Sometime ago I was meeting with a young couple preparing for marriage. In the course of our discussions, I became very concerned about some of the attitudes and priorities of the prospective groom. I felt I was obligated to express my concern. When I did so, I noticed that his fiancée was nodding her head rather vigorously in agreement. This caused me to have even more serious concerns. I wondered, and eventually asked her, whether she was holding back, avoiding the issue in order to keep peace. And that was indeed the case. I do not believe in that kind of peace.

I do not know whether you have ever heard Bishop Untener of Saginaw speak. He likes to use an overhead projector when he gives talks and enjoys belittling his own amateurish efforts at drawing. One time when he was speaking about the United States Bishops' pastoral *The Challenge of Peace: God's Promise and Our Response*, he put a transparency on the projector. It depicted two mountains separated by a short distance, with a little village of houses and a church at the base of each of them. He said the villagers always got along well with one another until a time the people of Village A thought that those in Village B were not doing their share of maintenance of the road that connected the two communities. Eventually, negotiations broke down. Then the leaders of Village A sent word to those in Village B: "Look up at your mountain."

At this point, Bishop Untener superimposed a second transparency and we saw a huge boulder on the peak of the mountain overlooking Village B. Then the villagers asked: "Will you do your share of the work now?" Another transparency. Now there was a boulder on the peak of the mountain overlooking Village A. Transparency followed transparency until there was a huge cluster of boulders on the top of each of the mountains.

Bishop Untener asked us to think about that for a minute. Is that any way to live? Even if none of those boulders ever comes crashing down and destroys the village and kills its people, that is certainly no way to live. Think of children growing up in that atmosphere of fear. Yet that is the atmosphere we and many of the people of the world have been living in for many years.

In the past several decades, the superpowers have embraced a policy something like that with nuclear weapons. Despite the recent agreements, the superpowers, with their arsenals of nuclear weapons, are capable of destroying each other. This policy is called *deterrence*. It includes the provision that each of these countries will have sufficient arms to destroy the other even after their own country has been effectively destroyed. That program is called Mutually Assured Destruction, or MAD for short. And madness it is. As the martyred Salvadoran Archbishop Oscar Romero said, "Peace is not the product of terror or fear." I simply cannot believe in that kind of peace.

In some of our city neighborhoods, grade school children know more about violence and guns than they do about peace, more about drugs than they do about nutrition, more about sex than about love and family life. We are in danger of rearing a generation that is illiterate in terms of peace and peaceful conflict resolution.

In the book of the prophet Jeremiah, we read that false prophets of that day cried, "Peace, peace," but there was no peace. I do not believe in a peace which is only a word.

But most of all, I would like to write about the peace I do believe in. The peace I believe in is a beautiful and many-faceted treasure. It includes peace with nature, expressed with reverence in some of the traditions of our native American. Pope John Paul II titled his 1990 New Year's message *Peace with All Creation*. Such a peace accepts the interrelationships and interdependence of all things on Earth and even beyond--the sun, the moon, and the stars.

The peace I believe in includes the simple life-style of the Amish people. As far as possible they use natural things and they use them gently. The peace I believe in is expressed not only in words but in the whole of one's life. We see this in many saints, notably in the life of St. Francis. He sensed a oneness and harmony in all of creation. He speaks of all creatures as one family. There are many appealing stories about Francis, about his relationship with animals, even wild ones. For him, they were not wild. And I am sure you are familiar with his prayer, "Lord, make me an instrument of your peace." The peace I believe in sees the Earth as Spaceship Earth with all of us interdependent and responsible for peace on Earth.

The peace I believe in begins with the creation story. Adam calls all of the animals before him and gives them their names. We read, also, that Adam and Eve are naked. They live in peace with the elements and do not need to be protected from a hostile environment. They are at peace with themselves, their bodies, and their sexuality. This is Paradise.

Sin means Paradise lost and peace lost. Yet, even after sin, there is exciting good news expressed in picturesque language. There will come a time when the wolf will be the guest of the lamb and the leopard will lie down with the kid. The peace I believe in means that warring peoples will beat their swords into plowshares and their spears into pruning hooks. And perhaps most beautiful of all, the peace I believe in looks to the day when nations will not train for war anymore. Is all this a dream? And if it is a dream, is it worthless? It is not worthless--not if we have faith. The peace I believe in is rooted in faith--the faith that Jesus says can move mountains can, in fact, do all things.

True peace recognizes...violence and is repelled by it, but also knows how to change it.

The peace I believe in is rooted not only in creation but also in redemption. It is a gift of grace, and, as our bishops say in their pastoral on peace, it calls for our response. Isaiah foretold the coming of a Prince of Peace, and at the birth of Jesus, the angels sang of peace on earth. After His resurrection, Jesus appeared to His disciples, and His first word to them was "Peace." Paradise regained--and more.

In the Easter Vigil, when we celebrate the rising of the Lord, an exultant church sings with poetic license: "O happy fault, O truly necessary sin of Adam, which gained for us so great a Redeemer." The peace I believe in is all-encompassing. It is peace with oneself, with one's body, with one's conscience. Peace with one's limitations and with one's talents. It also means peace with family, friends, and all other persons. Even if perfect agreement is not possible, the peace I believe in means accepting them for who and what they are.

The peace I believe in means, above all, peace with God. I am sure you have heard people say of someone who has recently died, "He made his peace with God." And our deep longing for peace expresses itself in the hopeful prayer, "May he/she rest in peace." These are beautiful expressions, and all this is possible only because of Jesus who is Himself our peace.

The peace I believe in is not blind to the violence, the truly terrible and frightening violence that still infects our world. True peace recognizes this violence and is repelled by it, but also knows how to change it. The peace I believe in is built on the commandment of Jesus: "You have heard that it was said 'You shall love your neighbor and hate your enemy.' But I say to you, love your enemies..." (Matthew 5:43-44).

How often in our world violence gives rise to further violence. I recall a cartoon from some years ago. A man is reprimanded by his superior at work. When he comes home, he takes out his repressed anger on his son. The son, in turn, kicks the family dog, which immediately begins to chase the cat. Violence gives rise to further violence. We believe that our sinfulness contributed to the violence that was heaped upon our Lord in His passion and death. Father John Shea, in reflecting on this, writes that in accepting His death Jesus says, in effect, that violence stops here. It stops with me. The peace I believe in is rooted in our redemption by Jesus.

The peace I believe in is treated at some length in *The Healing Power of Peace and Non-Violence*, a marvelous little book by Father Bernard Häring. I have seldom been so moved by a book as I have been by this one. The peace he describes is not simply a refusal to fight back: it is a healing. Isaiah the prophet, writing some seven hundred years before the time of Christ, wrote of a suffering servant whose suffering would be redemptive. By his stripes, Isaiah says, we are healed.

On the practical level, Father Häring develops in some detail the methods of civilian nonviolent defense and the steps to implement it. For the person of faith, peace is not an impossible dream.

The peace I believe in does not stand alone. It is built upon a foundation of justice. I have often told people that I have only one bumper sticker on my car. It is a quotation from Pope Paul VI: "If you want peace, work for justice." So long as people are deprived of what is rightfully theirs, the peace we seem to have is precarious. Pope John Paul II carries this one step further when he calls for a peace based on justice and love. If we want peace in our world, in our family, anywhere, we must be willing to work for justice. And we must love.

There is a story told of the Curé of Ars, St. John Vianney, when his bishop appointed him to Ars. The bishop said, "There is not much love there. You must bring it." We must do that in our world.

The peace I believe in sees the world as sacramental. To say that the world is sacramental is to say that because of Jesus who is *the* sacrament, all of nature can speak to us of God. A sacramental view of the world sees us and all of creation at peace. Peace flows like a river, nourishing and refreshing everything along its banks. A sacramental view sees nature and grace at peace. For this reason, when we gather for Liturgy, when we gather to celebrate the sacraments, we use things of nature and we use our bodies for speaking, singing, gesturing, and touching. The peace I believe in is celebrated and fostered in worship with others.

I wonder whether you ever read or hear something that makes you say, "Why, yes, of course! Why didn't I think of that?" I recently had such an experience when I read an article in which the author, Colman McCarthy, proposed that, beginning in first grade, we have courses in peace and nonviolent conflict resolution. It seems like such an obvious idea.

There is much more that could be said about the peace I believe in, but I am going to bring this letter to a close with one last thought. In the language that Jesus spoke, the word for peace is *Shalom*. *Shalom* means everything we mean by peace and more. *Shalom* almost has the sense of something physical coming down upon you. It includes every blessing from God. I once was talking with a Jewish storyteller. Yes, that is his profession and full-time occupation. In the course of our time together, we came around to discussing *Shalom*. He told me that although people commonly greeted one another with the single word *Shalom*, the full expression was *Shalom Alechem*, "Peace be with you." In responding, the other person inverts the order of the two words: *Alechem Shalom*, "And with you, peace." And the rabbis have an explanation for this: Inverting the order of the words is important, he said, because everything begins and ends with *Shalom*. I think of this when I use the solemn blessing at the end of the Eucharist:

> May the Lord bless you and keep you.
> May his face shine upon you and be gracious to you.
> May he look upon you with kindness
> And give you his peace.

Shalom Alechem!

Father Ed

QUESTIONS FOR REFLECTION AND DISCUSSION

1. Do you think that world peace is just an "impossible dream"? Why, or why not?
2. Pope Paul VI said, "If you want peace, work for justice." Discuss.
3. What are some things you can do to promote peace:

> *•In your family?*
> *•In your community?*
> *•In the world?*
> *•In the Church?*

18

THE EARTH I BELIEVE IN

Dear Friends,

Because the Earth and our environment is a topic of such interest and importance today, I am happy that so many people are showing an awareness and concern over the damage we are doing to planet Earth entrusted to us by God. There are many things about Earth and the environment that I do not believe in. I do not believe in an Earth that has an infinite capacity for abuse. I do not believe in an Earth that is one vast landfill, capable of absorbing all of our refuse and all of our contaminants indefinitely and not be damaged. I do not believe in an Earth whose resources are unlimited or can be replenished as rapidly as we can devise ways to consume them. I do not believe in an Earth where every wetland should be drained or filled and where every shoreland should be lined with houses and businesses. I do not believe in an Earth whose riches and beauty are ours to exploit without thought of those who will come after us.

There are many Earths I do not believe in, but I would rather reflect a little on the Earth I do believe in. That Earth is the creation of our loving God, and it still belongs to God. The Earth I believe in is the Earth of the psalmist who sings:

The LORD's is the Earth and its fullness;
 the world and those who dwell in it.

Psalm 24:1

The Earth I believe in is a word, it is the first self-revelation of our God. It is a kind of incarnation. It is a sign of the goodness, the beauty, the love, and the life-giving presence of God. It is sacramental.

In the story of creation, we read that God entrusted this Earth to Adam and Eve--and to all of us, their descendants. They were to cultivate and care for it. We, in turn, are to cultivate and care for it so that those who come after us can also enjoy its riches and its beauty. The world we pass on is an inheritance given to those who will follow. In the Great Law of the Haudenosaumee (Iroquois Confederacy), these Native Americans say, "In our every deliberation, we must consider the impact of our decisions on the next seven generations." Like them, we need to realize that we are stewards, not owners.

The Earth I believe in is not merely something that we live on or live in. We live with the Earth and we are called to live with it in peace.

The Earth I believe in is a delicate balance of uncounted organisms--of flowers and bees, of spiders and flies, of falcons and owls, of foxes and wolves, of cats and mice, and of literally millions of beautiful and exotic creatures. The Earth I believe in is a balance of sunshine and ozone filters, of melting snows, spring rains, and summer heat. It is a balance of night and day, of rest and growth, of a kind of death and rising in winter and summer. The Earth I believe in is an astonishingly complex interrelationship of living things, an ecosystem, marvelously resilient, and yet ever so fragile. Our well-being is inextricably tied to the health of this ecosystem.

The Earth I believe in is a gift and it comes gift-wrapped with a precious, life-sustaining blanket of air, which is itself a gift to be cherished. Someone has said that the destruction of clean air is impractical. What an understatement! People of faith ought to say more: We ought to say it is sinful!

Some cultures are closer to the Earth and appreciate our connectedness with the Earth better than we do. The Massai tribes of Africa, who live in land that is hot and dry, call God *Engai*. *Engai* is also their word for rain. And Thomas Merton, a city boy who, as a Trappist monk, grew close to nature as well as to grace, called rain a festival. Like the three young men who were thrown into the white-hot furnace, we, too, can pray: Fire and heat, dew and rain, frost and chill, ice and snow, lightnings and clouds, bless the Lord, praise and exalt God forever. (See Daniel 3:66-73.) On the Earth I believe in, all of these are festivals to be celebrated.

The Earth I believe in is like the Earth of the American Indian. An ancient Navajo prophecy holds that "if we dare to pollute the land and water, we will all suffer the consequences." I often recall the scene shown on television of an Indian riding to the brow of a hill and looking down at a stream polluted with rubbish. A tear wells up in his eye and flows down his cheek. This scene reminds me also of another American Indian, Chief Seattle.

In the 1850s, as the story goes, Chief Seattle responded to a request from the President of the United States to buy some of the tribal lands of his people. He said in part:

"The President in Washington sends word that he wishes to buy our land. But how can you buy or sell the sky? The land? The idea is strange to us. If we do not own the freshness of the air and the sparkle of the water, how can you buy them?...

"The rivers are our brothers. They quench our thirst. They carry our canoes and feed our children. So you must give to the rivers the kindness you would to any brother.

"If we sell you our land, remember that the air is precious to us, that the air shares its spirit with all the life it supports. The wind that gave our grandfather his first breath also receives his last sigh. The wind also gives our children the spirit of life....

"Will you teach your children what we have taught our children? That the earth is our mother?...

"Man did not weave the web of life, he is merely a strand in it. Whatever he does to the web, he does to himself.

"One thing we know, our god is also your god. The earth is precious to him and to harm the earth is to heap contempt on its creator.

"We love this earth as a newborn loves its mother's

heartbeat. So, if we sell you our land, love it as we have loved it. Care for it as we have cared for it. Hold in your mind the memory of the land as it is when you receive it. Preserve the land for all children and love it, as God loves us all....

"One thing we know: there is only one God. No man, be he Red Man or White Man, can be apart. We are brothers after all."

The Earth I believe in is vast, intricate, and interdependent. The poet Francis Thompson expressed this interdependence when he wrote that we cannot pluck a flower without troubling a star.

The earth I believe in is a cathedral, sacred space.

And the Earth and all of creation is holy. Another author, Mark Daughty, writes in *The Tablet*: "It is the whole of nature--from the protons to a Schubert sonata--which is glorified by the indwelling of God." We understand many things about the Earth I believe in, and we are constantly learning more. Yet there is always so much more that is beyond our understanding, that remains mystery. We know of atoms and subatomic particles. And now, I am told, scientists have learned that a single neuron, a highly specialized nerve cell, is as complicated as the brain. And the brain is a wonder we have only begun to comprehend.

The Earth I believe in challenges the best scientific minds and technology of our day. The experts tell us that we know so much and yet, we know so little. One researcher has said, for instance, that we haven't the faintest idea of how a fused sperm and egg differentiates itself internally to form all the organs of the human body.

As scientists continue to study all that has gone into the evolution of our world--the marvelous diversity of life-forms, the precise arrangement and balance of factors--they conclude that, scientifically speaking, it is statistically almost impossible that the world could have come to be by chance. As they reflect on these marvels, those who study begin to respond with awe and wonder. They begin to sound like the American Indians. The Indians sound like poets. The poets, in turn, sound like theologians, even mystics.

The Earth I believe in is truly wondrous and awesome. It is sacrament. It is grace. The Earth I believe in is a cathedral, sacred space. When we stand before a mountain, a volcano, the Grand Canyon or a waterfall, in a woods, on a river bank or a seashore, it is easy to think of God and to pray. The Earth I believe in is the Earth of St. Francis of Assisi. He sang of Brother Sun and Sister Moon. He loved the Earth and all of its inhabitants.

The Earth I believe in is a mother to the human body. The Earth is 71% salt water and 92 other elements. The human body is 71% salt water and the same 92 elements. The Earth I believe in is the matter from which we have been made. *Adamah*, the biblical name *Adam*, is not so much a proper name as a name for all humankind. We are all Adamah, of the Earth, earthlings. Our well-being is one with the well-being of our mother Earth. Our mother Earth first nurtures us; we, in turn, must nurture her.

The Earth I believe in, holy from the time of its creation, was raised higher, ennobled, divinized on the first Christmas when the Son of God took on our human nature and became the new Adamah. (See 1 Corinthians 15:45.) The Earth I believe in is now one with God-made-man in Jesus.

The Earth I believe in offers us the raw materials of things we use in worship. It provides us with wheat and grapes, and we bring these good gifts, transformed by human work into bread and wine, to the Eucharistic action. Here they become the Body and Blood of Christ. The Earth I believe in is truly worthy of wonder and awe--and of our love and care.

The Earth I believe in is also in trouble. We live on a "bridge over troubled waters"; we live on land that is becoming dangerously contaminated, and we often breathe unhealthful air. But I have hope for the Earth I believe in.

More and more people are becoming aware of our interdependence with our Earth. More and more people are beginning to speak out and to act to preserve the precious health of our Earth. More and more people are seeing the Earth as a divine trust. Pope John Paul II says that "an education in ecological responsibility is urgent" (*Peace with All Creation*, #12), and the bishops of the United States speak of "a new spirit of responsibility for the Earth" (*Renewing the Earth*, Part I C).

I hope and pray that the Earth I believe in may continue always to be a nourishing mother to us all. And may we be informed, responsible, loving, and caring children to her.

Peace!

Father Ed

QUESTIONS FOR REFLECTION AND DISCUSSION

1. What do you understand by the statement that the Earth is a sacrament?
2. How would our Earth be different if we all adopted the practice of the Iroquois in making decisions?
3. What is being done to preserve the environment in your community? What can you personally do?

19

THE FORGIVENESS I BELIEVE IN

Dear Friends,

Occasionally in my contacts with parishioners and friends, the subject of forgiveness comes up. It is something we all have to deal with frequently--in our marriage, with our children, relatives and neighbors, at work. And it is never easy to forgive. Sometimes, after I have talked with people about this, I have thought that I should sit down and write, in an organized way, about what I think of forgiveness.

First, let me say something about the forgiveness I don't believe in. I don't believe in a forgiveness which is withheld until the other person has paid for the offense. Or a forgiveness that is not willing to forget. I remember a marriage counselor telling me about a couple with whom she was working. She said they both have long memories. Every time a problem arises, they go back to all kinds of earlier hurts, events from years ago, apologized for and forgiven many times over. I don't believe in those kinds of forgiveness.

The forgiveness I do believe in is most beautifully portrayed by Jesus in the parable of the Prodigal Son. The story appears in the fifteenth chapter of the Gospel according to Luke. The reading as we have it in the liturgy gives the very beginning of the chapter and this, friends, is very important. It begins by stating that the tax collectors and sinners were all gathering about Jesus to hear Him, at which the

Pharisees and Scribes murmured, "This man welcomes sinners and eats with them." Our Sunday reading then omits about eight verses which include the story of the lost sheep and the lost coin. It continues with this parable, which is sometimes called the story of the Prodigal Father and sometimes the parable of the Lost Son.

Jesus begins the story by saying, "A man had two sons." Right away, we need to be aware that we are going to be one or possibly both of those sons. Or should I say daughters? The younger of them said to his father, "Father, give me the share of your estate that should come to me." So the father divided up the property. A few days later this younger son collected all his belongings and went off to a distant land where he squandered his money on dissolute living. It is important to understand that it was not improper in the Jewish culture for a son to ask for his share of the estate. He was not, however, to spend it before his father's death, so that if the father would ever be in need, the son would be able to help him. We now have the picture of the problem.

The younger son has left his father, who, in the story, is God the Father. The son has also left his brother. If we want to transpose this to the context of today, we might say that he has left the Christian community. He has left his homeland. For the Jew, we remember, that is the land that was promised first of all to Abraham and acquired through God's assistance. Even today, we call it the Holy Land. So this son has not merely done one or two things; he has taken on a totally different way of life. He squandered his possessions, also translated as "his inheritance." This means that he has, in effect, renounced his sonship. By his actions, he has said that he no longer wants to a part of the community that is God's family.

We read that after he has spent everything, a great famine breaks out in the land where he is living, and he is in dire need. Then, we are told, he hires himself out to a landowner who sends him to his farm to care for the pigs. He longs to fill his belly with food given to the pigs, but no one offers him anything.

I once heard a Scripture scholar comment on this. He

said that in the Jewish mind there are three kinds or categories of sinners. The first is the Jew who is basically faithful but who has sinned and is now repentant. God's mercy is his. The second is the Gentile. In the mind of the Jew, he is simply outside the embrace of God's mercy. The third is the worst kind of sinner. This is the Jew who rejects his faith and assumes the life-style of the Gentiles. In our story, that is what the young man has done. He is living with Gentiles and is taking care of pigs.

Jesus continues the story, saying, "Coming to his senses...." Isn't that interesting? "Coming to his senses...." In the Scriptures, wisdom is following the path of God, and it is the fool who says in his heart that there is no God. This son is beginning to experience conversion. But it is only a beginning. In our childhood catechisms, this would be imperfect contrition. He thinks to himself, How many hired hands at my father's place have more than enough to eat while here I am starving? I will break away and return to my father and say to him--and he rehearses a confession--"Father, I have sinned against heaven and against you. I no longer deserve to be called your son. Treat me as you would treat one of your hired workers." With that he sets out for his father's house.

The story continues: While he was still a long way off, his father caught sight of him and was deeply moved. "A long way off." This tells us that the father must have been watching for him. When he saw him, he was deeply moved. That happens only when someone cares. Then, Jesus says, the father did an amazing thing. The father ran out to meet him. In the Jewish tradition, the father never ran out like that to meet any of his children. This father did and threw his arms around him and kissed him.

The son began his confession, "Father, I have sinned against God and against you. I no longer deserve to be called your son." But before he can complete his confession, his father interrupts him. He calls to his servants, "Quickly bring out the finest robe and put it on him; put a ring on his finger and sandals on his feet." This is never done for a servant; these are signs of sonship. The father continues, "Take the fatted calf and slaughter it. Then let us celebrate with a feast because this son of mine was dead and has come to life again; he was lost and has been found."

Meanwhile, the elder son is coming in from the fields and hears the sounds of the celebration. He calls one of the servants and asks him the reason for the music and dancing. The servant tells him that his brother has returned and the father has ordered that the fatted calf be killed because of his joy at having him back in good health. The elder son grows angry at this and will not go in to the celebration. Once again, it is the father who goes out to a son to plead with him. The son says to his father, "Look, all these years I served you and not once did I disobey your orders; yet you never gave me even a young goat to feast on with my friends. But when your son [notice that he will not even call him his brother] returns who swallowed up your property with prostitutes, for him you slaughter the fattened calf." The father replies, "My son, you are with me always; everything I have is yours. But now we must celebrate and rejoice, because your brother [and the father insists that he is a brother, a member of the family] was dead and has come back to life again; he was lost and has been found."

This God watches over us, not to catch us but to wait for our return.

The forgiveness I believe in is that of a forgiving God, who goes beyond all human customs and expectations. This God watches over us, not to catch us but to wait for our return. The message of this parable, however, is not only about God and forgiveness but also about us and forgiveness. We are to be forgiving like God. We need to learn to forgive not only others but also ourselves.

You may recall how in the Gospel we are told to be perfect as our heavenly Father is perfect. That is in the Gospel according to Matthew. In the parallel passage in the Gospel according to Luke the statement is somewhat different. We are to be merciful as our heavenly Father is merciful. Wouldn't it be a wonderful world if all of us were?

Peace!

Father Ed

QUESTIONS FOR REFLECTION AND DISCUSSION

1. This parable is usually called the parable of the Prodigal Son. Do you think it is more about the son or more about God the Father? Why?
2. Jesus told this parable in response to criticism. Of whom is the parable itself a criticism?
3. Do you think this parable is dangerous because it is too easy on sinners?

20

THE LOVE I BELIEVE IN

Dear Friends,

I hope that you will believe me when I say that I have wanted to write this letter for some time. I have delayed doing so, not because I have been too busy. Rather, I have been hesitant because I have not felt sure about how to approach the subject. It's about love. Like most of my other letters, it will be not so much a theological treatment as a reflection on things I have seen and experienced in my parish ministry.

On the one hand, there are loves that I have seen and that I must say I don't believe in. I don't believe in a love that tries to possess another person. Such a love binds and imprisons; it limits and stifles. It does not give life or growth or freedom or joy--to either the lover or the beloved.

On the other hand, and I am talking here about human love, I do not believe in a love that seems always to be perfectly unselfish. A love that never gets angry or irritable. A love that is always giving, always smiling, always happy. Human love in the real world always falls short of perfection, and yet I believe that it can truly be called love.

I do not believe in a love that is so busy doing things that it never has time just to be. A love that gives everything that is wanted even though that may not be good for the beloved. I do not believe in a love that gives every *thing* but does not give itself. Love is essentially a giving of self.

I do not believe in a love that will never bring pain, even when that pain would be the birth pangs of new and richer life.

There are many loves that I do not believe in, but most of all, there is a love I do believe in. The love I believe in sometimes brings together a man and woman, and a marriage is formed. This love often gives birth to new persons and it brings these infant persons along in life, ultimately to maturity. And, then, when that time comes, the love I believe in sets them free.

This love, like all love, is really a relationship. It is a deep and special relationship that shows itself in words of endearment, of support, of affirmation. This love shows itself also in actions of tenderness, in touches, in kisses, in embrace. In marriage, the ultimate celebration of this love is sexual intercourse.

The love I believe in not only gives life but also sustains and fosters it. I would like to illustrate this from a story I've read. It is presented as a true story. After the settlement treaty in Korea in the fifties, there were thousands of orphans in that devastated land. Orphan homes were quickly set up to care for these homeless children. Two of these homes were established in villages not far apart. They were similar in all respects except that the one had twice as many nurses and assistants for the same number of children. The death rate in the home with the fewer nurses was twice as high as that in the other. The growth rate of those who did live was measurably slower, both physically and mentally. The only discernible difference in the care of those children was this: In the home where they had more nurses, the children were touched and held and talked to much more. They received more of the signs of love. The love I believe in nourishes and fosters life.

The love I believe in heals. We hear frequently about faith healing. We should talk also about love healing. I have seen it. A loving touch, a loving look, a loving word can heal bodies and spirits.

Jean Vanier, founder of L'Arche Communities in which helpers live with severely handicapped persons, tells this story: "In Rome we welcomed into L'Arche a beautiful little boy called Armando. He was born with a very severe handicap. His mother could not cope. So she put Armando into an orphanage. When a child senses that it is not loved and feels unwanted, there is a wound in its heart. So it was that Armando refused to eat. There was too much anguish and inner pain. We were asked if we could welcome him into our community. So he came to us. And there in that very small home where there were just four children, he was held, he was loved, he was bathed, he was fed. And gradually he began to taste communion. He began to like being loved, and one day he opened his heart and, somewhere inside him, he decided to live. And so today, if you come, you will find Armando. He is now seven years old, tiny: He has not grown. Yet if you take him in your arms, his eyes light up and a smile appears on his face and he looks at you, and all his body quivers and says 'I love you.' He says it not with words but with his little body. He has found communion and he is living it. Armando wants neither money nor power nor work nor knowledge. All he wants is another heart."

And, sadly, I think of another boy, Andy, whom I came to know many years ago. I do not know how this story ends because his family moved away, but this much I do know. Andy was the second son born to a fine young couple who eventually had five children. Andy was born prematurely and spent his first months in an incubator. When his parents finally brought their still tiny infant home, they were told not to hold or handle him any more than necessary. And so, little Andy was not held, cuddled, kissed, played with, as every little child should be.

As Andy developed and began to play with his brother and sisters, he frequently was troublesome and was sent to his room as a punishment. As he grew older, his antisocial behavior became more serious. The last I heard, years ago, was that psychiatrists thought his problems stemmed from the lack of physical love and contact in his early life. Their conclusion was that Andy would never be able to live peaceably in society unless someone could work with him and love him for so long that he could no longer deny that he is lovable. The love I believe in heals.

The love I believe in also gets hands dirty, its own hands! And it gets the whole body tired, its own body. The love I believe in is not always romantic. It is sometimes wiping up spilled milk--milk spilled by an infant or an old person or even anyone in between. It is sometimes holding a door, sometimes holding a hand. It is sometimes giving a smile, sometimes giving a meal. It is sometimes giving consolation, sometimes giving a gentle teasing. Sometimes it is just sitting there and being with.

Love has special ears. It also has special eyes.

The love I believe in sometimes talks and shares and reveals itself. But the love I believe in also listens, and, when it listens, it hears not only words but feelings and needs as well. Love has special ears. It also has special eyes.

The love I believe in builds bridges and opens doors and windows--most of all between persons. The love I believe in knows that persons are not things. Persons can give themselves and be received but they can never be taken or fully possessed. And love is able to let go when letting go is for the good of the beloved. The love I believe in knows that to reach out in love is to be vulnerable, but it continues to reach out because that is the only way to live. To live is to live in relationships.

The love I believe in weathers winters because it hopes for springs, in seasons and between persons. The love I believe in sometimes writes poetry, sings songs, paints pictures, and dances. The love I believe in can laugh with those who laugh, weep with those who weep, die with those who die, and wait with those who wait. There is a time for every season under heaven, and love takes the time.

The love I believe in has imagination and a twinkle in its eye. It delights in surprises, is quick to laugh--at things, at self, and, sometimes, but gently, at others. The love I believe in is playful.

The love I believe in has a sense of wonder and awe. It can spend time quietly in the presence of the beauty of nature: a sunset, a sumac bush, a maple tree, new-fallen snow and, above all, a newborn child. The love I believe in is contemplative in the presence of beauty and reverent in the presence of life.

The love I believe in loves the beloved as is, yet challenges the beloved to become all that she or he can be. When necessary, the love I believe in, like the God I believe in, rebukes but does so gently. In this way, too, love gives new life.

Love has many degrees. It is, in us, always imperfect, and yet, even though imperfect, a work of art. And the perfecting of that work of art takes time, imagination, perseverance--and grace. We had a banner one time at our parish with the expression, printed as one long misspelled word: *loveisahelluvalotawork*. No matter how you spell it, that is true.

The love I believe in has many faces. It has the face of young lovers who have so much to talk about, so much to reveal and learn. Young lovers who are sure no one has ever loved as they do. Young lovers who are certain they will always be in love like this and, because of this, will always be happy. Love has the face of those who are older, who have loved for some years. And it has the face of the elderly, perhaps deeply wrinkled now, but still very much alive. Love is quieter here, seasoned with experiences, purified in sufferings and sacrifices, deepened as it has been given and received, sustained in memories and hopes, secure even in silence.

Love has the face of a parent, and love has the face of a child. Love has the face of a friend, of any age and of either sex, who loves us as we are and continues to love us into what we can become. Love can have as many faces as there are people on earth and, whatever its face, it loves us into personhood and wholeness so that we, in turn, can love and give to others.

And the love I believe in has yet another face. It is the

face of God--the God who first loves us into being. The God who, in the thousand pages of the Bible, really speaks only this one word, *love*. The God described by Hosea as one who will not punish or abandon us in our unfaithfulness, but who will take us back because God is God and not human. The God whose face we see in Jesus, and who gives us the ultimate sign of love: Greater love than this no one has than that he lay down his life for a friend. Love has the face of the God who wants only one thing from us, who reduces all commandments to one: that we love as this God loves, the God of whom St. John could write, "God is love and whoever remains in love remains in God and God in [that person]" (1 John 4:15).

May you and I, friends, and all people abide, live in love. Peace!

Father Ed

QUESTIONS FOR REFLECTION AND DISCUSSION

1. What do you think "tough love" means? Is it true love? Why or why not?
2. A special kind of love is the love of friendship. Is friendship "ahelluvalotawork"? Discuss.
3. Can you think of stories of love healing?

21

THE CANA I BELIEVE IN

Dear Friends,

The Gospel this past Sunday was about the wedding at Cana. It is such an appealing story, and it has been a favorite of mine for a long time. I have also, over the years, become aware of the fact that there is much more to this story than I saw in it at first. It is filled with hints of more, with evocative, symbolic references. In my homily, I challenged the assembly to work along with me to seek to find some of those deeper hidden meanings. Comments I received after Mass indicated that people understood and appreciated the challenge.

The Scriptures often say more than appears on the surface. This is especially true of the Gospel according to St. John in which we find the story of the wedding at Cana. This story is a particularly rich example of deeper meanings, and I would like to tell you something of what I said in my homily. Following along will take some effort--more than the comics or even the front page of the newspaper requires, but I think you will find it not only interesting but also rewarding. John gives us a number of indications that he wants us to think of another event while we are reading about this one. That other event is the passion, death, and resurrection of our Lord.

Unfortunately, the first of these hints is not in the reading as we have it in the Sunday Gospel. It is found in four words immediately preceding the reading. When the scholars put together our lectionary, our book of liturgical readings from the Bible, they selected the passages and began and ended them where they chose. The four important words immediately before our passage are, "On the third day."

I suspect that you are thinking, What could be so important about those few words? Let me explain. In the first chapter of John's Gospel account, we have the expression "the next day" three times. This story follows immediately, at the beginning of the second chapter. Its opening words are, "On the third day." As my computer-literate friends would say, that does not compute. It does not compute if we are thinking in terms of calendar time. But that is not what it is about; it is a theological statement. With a little help from the Scripture scholars, we see that the third day in the Scriptures is always a day of deliverance.

There are quite a few examples, and I am sure you will recognize some of them. For instance, think of the story of Jonah inside the huge fish. On the third day he was spat out upon the shore. And we all know that Easter Sunday is the third day after Good Friday. Good Friday and Easter Sunday. That is the connection John wants us to make at the very beginning of this story. If we catch this, we will more likely catch the other hints. On this third day, at this wedding, Mary tells Jesus that the newly married couple has run out of wine. Jesus responds, "Woman, how does your concern affect me? My hour has not yet come" (John 2:4).

Two words in that response are important for our understanding of the deeper meaning we are after. They are *woman* and *hour*. First, *woman*. Isn't that a strange way for a son to address his mother? Scripture commentators tell us that in that culture it simply was not done. John uses it here because he wants us to be struck by its strangeness. Then, if we are struck, he hopes we will recall that there is another time when Jesus uses the same word to address His mother. It is when He is hanging on the cross. Again, we are directed to think of Good Friday.

The second key word is *hour*. Jesus says: "My hour has not yet come." Here, too, John is tying this moment to the passion, death, and resurrection of the Lord. As Jesus is about to enter His Passover through death to glory, at the Last Supper, He prays, "Father, the hour has come" (John 17:1).

These two words, then, *woman* and *hour,* are used by John to help us relate this wedding celebration to the events at the end of Jesus' life on earth. I hope that you are still with me! John now describes the scene that follows. Jesus picks out six stone water jars and directs the servants to fill them with water. These jars were there for Jewish ceremonial washings, washings which were a part of the Old Covenant, the Old Testament. Jesus changes the water into wine. Again John wants us to think of the Last Supper. At the Last Supper, Jesus changes wine into His own blood, the blood of the new and eternal covenant. When the headwaiter tastes the water-made-wine, he says that this new wine is better. The New Covenant in the blood of Jesus is a fulfillment of the Old.

John calls this a sign. Sacraments, we remember, are signs. It is through the sacraments, friends, that you and I enter into that new covenant, our relationship with God. It is through the sacrament of the Eucharist that we, here and now, celebrate and renew our covenant, our union, communion with God and one another. Are you still with me?

There is one more idea, a rather big one. This will help tie everything together. John says at the end of this event, "Jesus did this as the beginning of His signs in Cana in Galilee...and His disciples began to believe in him"(John 2:11).

A few chapters later, we read, "[Now] this was the second sign Jesus did when He came to Galilee from Judea" (John 4:54). John tells us that this also was in Cana, and he uses these two events to frame a picture, to show a unity in this entire section. In between these two signs in Cana, in the center of this picture, we meet John the Baptist. Here, the Baptist repeats what he's said earlier, "I am not the Messiah." Then he says, "The one who has the bride is the bridegroom; [Here's wedding talk again!] the best man, who stands and listens for him, rejoices greatly at the bridegroom's voice. So, this joy of mine has been made complete" (John 3:29).

So, Jesus is the groom and John the Baptist is the best man. But this leaves us without a bride! Who is the bride? All of us! That is what Isaiah says in this Sunday's first reading:

God will take His people as His bride. For us, our marriage to God is a New Covenant sealed in the blood of Christ. We, as a people, are the bride of Christ. We are united with God in Jesus in a marriage relationship, a loving, faithful, lifelong covenantal relationship.

Over my years as a parish priest, I have seen wonderful examples of faithfulness and love, sometimes heroic dedication, in marriage. But Jesus is infinitely more than a human spouse. He loves perfectly, unconditionally--no strings attached. He loves us "no matter what."

Sometimes in parishes couples ask us to celebrate with them their wedding anniversary, a twenty-fifth, a fiftieth. In these celebrations, they thank God for their years together and often they renew their commitment to one another. When we think of our marriage covenant with Christ, the Eucharist is our thanksgiving, and in the communion of the Body and Blood of Christ we renew our covenant-commitment.

So, we conclude as we began, by saying that this Gospel is about a wedding. But now we see that it is not only about a wedding of a couple in Cana two thousand years ago. The bride and groom are unnamed so that we can insert our names because the story is really about today, it is about here and now, it is about us! The wedding is ours!

I think you can see why I like this story so much! It is a story not only for couples, a story about marriage in the usual sense. It is a story for all of us who have been chosen by Jesus to be His bride. And we know that His love has no limits.

Congratulations on *your* marriage!

Peace!

Father Ed

QUESTIONS FOR REFLECTION OR DISCUSSION

1. Does understanding the wedding at Cana story in this way make it a richer experience for you? Does it take anything away? Explain.
2. How can this understanding enrich your participation in the Eucharist?